THE WORLD 100 YEARS AGO

D1415061

PARIS

THE WORLD 100 YEARS AGO

BERLIN

EGYPT

THE CITIES OF JAPAN

LONDON

MOSCOW

PARIS

PEKING

SOUTHERN ITALY

BURTON HOLMES

PARIS

—

Fred L. Israel
General Editor

Arthur M. Schlesinger, Jr.
Senior Consulting Editor

CHELSEA HOUSE PUBLISHERS
Philadelphia

CHELSEA HOUSE PUBLISHERS

EDITOR-IN-CHIEF Stephen Reginald
MANAGING EDITOR James D. Gallagher
PRODUCTION MANAGER Pamela Loos
ART DIRECTOR Sara Davis
PICTURE EDITOR Judy Hasday
SENIOR PRODUCTION EDITOR Lisa Chippendale
ASSOCIATE ART DIRECTOR Takeshi Takahashi
COVER DESIGN Dave Loose Design

First Printing

1 3 5 7 9 8 6 4 2

Library of Congress Cataloging-in-Publication Data

Holmes, Burton, b. 1870
Paris/Burton Holmes; Fred L. Israel, general editor;
Arthur M. Schlesinger, jr., senior consulting editor.
    p.   cm. — (The world 100 years ago today)
Includes index.

ISBN 0-7910-4662-1 (hc). — ISBN 0-7910-4663-X (pbk.)

1. Holmes, Burton, b. 1870—Journeys—France—Paris.
2. Paris (France)—Description and travel. 3. Paris
(France)—Buildings, structures, etc.—Pictorial works.
4. Paris (France)—Intellectual life—19th century. I.
Israel, Fred L. II Schlesinger, Arthur Meier, 1917- . III.
Title. IV. Series.
DC707.H716   1997
914.4'360481—dc21   97-36085
                                                   CIP

CONTENTS

The Great Globe Trotter   6
Irving Wallace

Burton Holmes   24
Arthur M. Schlesinger, jr.

The World 100 Years Ago   26
Dr. Fred Israel

Paris   35

Further Reading   138

Contributors   139

Index   140

THE GREAT GLOBE TROTTER

By Irving Wallace

One day in the year 1890, Miss Nellie Bly, of the *New York World,* came roaring into Brooklyn on a special train from San Francisco. In a successful effort to beat Phileas Fogg's fictional 80 days around the world, Miss Bly, traveling with two handbags and flannel underwear, had circled the globe in 72 days, 6 hours, and 11 minutes. Immortality awaited her.

Elsewhere that same year, another less-publicized globe-girdler made his start toward immortality. He was Mr. Burton Holmes, making his public debut with slides and anecdotes ("Through Europe With a Kodak") before the Chicago Camera Club. Mr. Holmes, while less spectacular than his feminine rival, was destined, for that very reason, soon to dethrone her as America's number-one traveler.

Today, Miss Bly and Mr. Holmes have one thing in common: In the mass mind they are legendary vagabonds relegated to the dim and dusty past of the Iron Horse and the paddle-wheel steamer. But if Miss Bly, who shuffled off this mortal coil in 1922, is now only a part of our folklore, there are millions to testify that

Mr. Burton Holmes, aged seventy-six, is still very much with us.

Remembering that Mr. Holmes was an active contemporary of Miss Bly's, that he was making a livelihood at traveling when William McKinley, John L. Sullivan, and Admiral Dewey ruled the United States, when Tony Pastor, Lily Langtry, and Lillian Russell ruled the amusement world, it is at once amazing and reassuring to pick up the daily newspapers of 1946 and find, sandwiched between advertisements of rash young men lecturing on "Inside Stalin" and "I Was Hitler's Dentist," calm announcements that tomorrow evening Mr. Burton Holmes has something more to say about "Beautiful Bali."

Burton Holmes, a brisk, immaculate, chunky man with gray Vandyke beard, erect bearing, precise speech ("folks are always mistaking me for Monty Woolley," he says, not unhappily), is one of the seven wonders of the entertainment world. As Everyman's tourist, Burton Holmes has crossed the Atlantic Ocean thirty times, the Pacific Ocean twenty times, and has gone completely around the world six times. He has spent fifty-five summers abroad, and recorded a half million feet of film of those summers. He was the first person to take motion picture cameras into Russia and Japan. He witnessed the regular decennial performance of the Passion Play at Oberammergau in 1890, and attended the first modern Olympics at Athens in 1896. He rode on the first Trans-Siberian train across Russia, and photographed the world's first airplane meet at Rheims.

As the fruit of these travels, Burton Holmes has delivered approximately 8,000 illustrated lectures that have grossed, according to an estimate by *Variety,* five million dollars in fifty-three winters. Because he does not like to be called a lecturer—"I'm a performer," he insists, "and I have performed on more legitimate stages than platforms"—he invented the word "travelogue" in London to describe his activity.

His travelogues, regarded as a fifth season of the year in most communities, have won him such popularity that he holds the record for playing in the longest one-man run in American show business. In the five and a half decades past, Burton Holmes has successively met the hectic competition of big-time vaudeville, stage, silent pictures, radio, and talking pictures, and he has survived them all.

At an age when most men have retired to slippered ease or are hounded by high blood pressure, Burton Holmes is more active and more popular than ever before. In the season just finished, which he started in San Francisco during September, 1945, and wound up in New York during April, 1946, Holmes appeared in 187 shows, a record number. He averaged six travelogues a week, spoke for two hours at each, and did 30 percent more box-office business than five years ago. Not once was a scheduled lecture postponed or canceled. In fact, he has missed only two in his life. In 1935, flying over the Dust Bowl, he suffered laryngitis and was forced to bypass two college dates. He has never canceled an appearance before a paid city audience. Seven years ago, when one of his elderly limbs was fractured in an automobile crack-up in Finland, there was a feeling that Burton Holmes might not make the rounds. When news of the accident was released, it was as if word had gone out that Santa Claus was about to cancel his winter schedule. But when the 1939 season dawned, Burton Holmes rolled on the stage in a wheelchair, and from his seat of pain (and for 129 consecutive appearances thereafter), he delivered his travel chat while 16-mm film shimmered on the screen beside him.

Today, there is little likelihood that anything, except utter extinction, could keep Holmes from his waiting audiences. Even now, between seasons, Holmes is in training for his next series— 150 illustrated lectures before groups in seventeen states.

Before World War II, accompanied by Margaret Oliver, his wife of thirty-two years, Holmes would spend his breathing spells on summery excursions through the Far East or Europe. While aides captured scenery on celluloid, Holmes wrote accompanying lecture material in his notebooks. Months later, he would communicate his findings to his cult, at a maximum price of $1.50 per seat. With the outbreak of war, Holmes changed his pattern. He curtailed travel outside the Americas. This year, except for one journey to Las Vegas, Nevada, where he personally photographed cowboy cutups and shapely starlets at the annual Helldorado festival, Holmes has been allowing his assistants to do all his traveling for him.

Recently, one crew, under cameraman Thayer Soule, who helped shoot the Battle of Tarawa for the Marines, brought Holmes a harvest of new film from Mexico. Another crew, after four months in Brazil last year, and two in its capital this year, returned to Holmes with magnificent movies. Meantime, other crews, under assignment from Holmes, are finishing films on Death Valley, the West Indies, and the Mississippi River.

In a cottage behind his sprawling Hollywood hilltop home, Holmes is busy, day and night, sorting the incoming negative, cutting and editing it, and rewriting lectures that will accompany the footage this winter. He is too busy to plan his next trip. Moreover, he doesn't feel that he should revisit Europe yet. "I wouldn't mind seeing it," he says, "but I don't think my public would be interested. My people want a good time, they want escape, they want sweetness and light, beauty and charm. There is too much rubble and misery over there now, and I'll let those picture magazines and Fox Movietone newsreels show all that. I'll wait until it's tourist time again."

When he travels, he thinks he will visit three of the four accessible places on earth that he has not yet seen. One is Tahiti, which he barely missed a dozen times, and the other two are Iran and Iraq. The remaining country that he has not seen, and has no wish to see, is primitive Afghanistan. Of all cities on earth, he would most like to revisit Kyoto, once capital of Japan. He still recalls that the first movies ever made inside Japan were ones he made in Kyoto, in 1899. The other cities he desires to revisit are

Venice and Rome. The only island for which he has any longing is Bali—"the one quaint spot on earth where you can really get away from it all."

In preparing future subjects, Holmes carefully studies the success of his past performances. Last season, his two most popular lectures in the East were "California" and "Adventures in Mexico." The former grossed $5,100 in two Chicago shows; the latter jammed the St. Louis Civic Auditorium with thirty-five hundred potential señores and señoritas. Holmes will use these subjects again, with revisions, next season, and add some brand-new Latin American and United States topics. He will sidestep anything relating to war. He feels, for example, that anything dealing with the once exotic Pacific islands might have a questionable reception—"people will still remember those white crosses they saw in newsreels of Guadalcanal and Iwo Jima."

Every season presents its own obstacles, and the next will challenge Holmes with a new audience of travel-sated and disillusioned ex-GI's. Many of these men, and their families, now know that a South Sea island paradise means mosquitoes and malaria and not Melville's Fayaway and Loti's Rarahu. They know Europe means mud and ruins and not romance. Nevertheless, Holmes is confident that he will win these people over.

"The veterans of World War II will come to my travelogues just as their fathers did. After the First World War, I gave illustrated lectures on the sights of France, and the ex-doughboys enjoyed them immensely. But I suppose there's no use comparing that war to this. The First World War was a minor dispute between gentlemen. In this one, the atrocities and miseries will be difficult to forget. I know I can't give my Beautiful Italy lecture next season to men who know Italy only as a pigsty, but you see, in my heart Italy is forever beautiful, and I see things in Italy they can't see, poor fellows. How could they? . . . Still, memory is frail, and one day these boys will forget and come to my lectures not to hoot but to relive the better moments and enjoy themselves."

While Burton Holmes prepares his forthcoming shows, his business manager, a slightly built dynamo named Walter Everest, works on next season's bookings. Everest contacts organizations interested in sponsoring a lecture series, arranges dates and prices, and often leases auditoriums on his own. Everest concentrates on cities where Holmes is known to be popular, Standing Room Only cities like New York, Boston, Philadelphia, Chicago, Los Angeles. On the other hand, he is cautious about the cities where Holmes has been unpopular in the past—Toledo, Cleveland, Indianapolis, Cincinnati. The one city Holmes now avoids entirely is Pomona, California, where, at a scheduled Saturday matinee, he found himself facing an almost empty house. The phenomenon of a good city or a poor city is inexplicable. In rare cases, there may be a reason for failure, and then Holmes will attempt to resolve it. When San Francisco was stone-deaf to Holmes, investigation showed that he had been competing with the annual opera season. Last year, he rented a theater the week before the opera began. He appeared eight times and made a handsome profit.

Once Holmes takes to the road for his regular season, he is a perpetual-motion machine. Leaving his wife behind, he barnstorms with his manager, Everest, and a projectionist, whirling to Western dates in his Cadillac, making long hops by plane, following the heavier Eastern circuit by train. Holmes likes to amaze younger men with his activities during a typical week. If he speaks in Detroit on a Tuesday night, he will lecture in Chicago on Wednesday evening, in Milwaukee on Thursday, be back in Chicago for Friday evening and a Saturday matinee session, then go on to Kansas City on Sunday, St. Louis on Monday, and play a return engagement in Detroit on Tuesday.

This relentless merry-go-round (with Saturday nights off to attend a newsreel "and see what's happening in the world") invigorates Holmes, but grinds his colleagues to a frazzle. One morning last season, after weeks of trains and travel, Walter

Everest was awakened by a porter at six. He rose groggily, sat swaying on the edge of his berth trying to put on his shoes. He had the look of a man who had pushed through the Matto Grosso on foot. He glanced up sleepily, and there, across the aisle, was Holmes, fully dressed, looking natty and refreshed. Holmes smiled sympathetically. "I know, Walter," he said, "this life is tiring. One day both of us ought to climb on some train and get away from it all."

In his years on the road, Holmes has come to know his audience thoroughly. He is firm in the belief that it is composed mostly of traveled persons who wish to savor the glamorous sights of the world again. Through Burton, they relive their own tours. Of the others, some regard a Holmes performance as a preview. They expect to travel; they want to know the choice sights for their future three-month jaunt to Ecuador. Some few, who consider themselves travel authorities, come to a Holmes lecture to point out gleefully the good things that he missed. "It makes them happy," Holmes says cheerfully. Tomorrow's audience, for the most, will be the same as the one that heard the Master exactly a year before. Generations of audiences inherit Holmes, one from the other.

An average Holmes lecture combines the atmosphere of a revival meeting and a family get-together at which home movies are shown. A typical Holmes travelogue begins in a brightly lit auditorium, at precisely three minutes after eight-thirty. The three minutes is to allow for latecomers. Holmes, attired in formal evening clothes, strides from the wings to center stage. People applaud; some cheer. Everyone seems to know him and to know exactly what to expect. Holmes smiles broadly. He is compact, proper, handsome. His goatee dominates the scene. He has worn it every season, with the exception of one in 1895 (when, beardless, he somewhat resembled Paget's Sherlock Holmes). Now, he speaks crisply. He announces that this is the third lecture of his fifty-fourth season. He announces his subject—"Adventures in Mexico."

He walks to one side of the stage, where a microphone is standing. The lights are dimmed. The auditorium becomes dark. Beyond the fifth row, Holmes cannot be seen. The all-color 16-mm film is projected on the screen. The film opens, minus title and credits, with a shot through the windshield of an automobile speeding down the Pan-American Highway to Monterrey. Holmes himself is the sound track. His speech, with just the hint of a theatrical accent, is intimate, as if he were talking in a living room. He punctuates descriptive passages with little formal jokes. When flowers and orange trees of Mexico are on the screen, he says, "We have movies and talkies, but now we should have smellies and tasties"—and he chuckles.

The film that he verbally captions is a dazzling, uncritical montage of Things Mexican. There is a señora selling tortillas, and close-ups of how tortillas are made. There is a bullfight, but not the kill. There is snow-capped Popocatepetl, now for sale at the bargain price of fifteen million dollars. There are the pyramids outside Mexico City, older than those of Egypt, built by the ancient Toltecs who went to war with wooden swords so that they would not kill their enemies.

Holmes's movies and lectures last two hours, with one intermission. The emphasis is on description, information, and oddity. Two potential ingredients are studiously omitted. One is adventure, the other politics. Holmes is never spectacular. "I want nothing dangerous. I don't care to emulate the explorers, to risk my neck, to be the only one or the first one there. Let others tackle the Himalayas, the Amazon, the North Pole, let them break the trails for me. I'm just a Cook's tourist, a little ahead of the crowd, but not too far ahead." Some years ago, Holmes did think that he was an explorer, and became very excited about it, he now admits sheepishly. This occurred in a trackless sector of Northern Rhodesia. Holmes felt that he had discovered a site never before seen by an outsider. Grandly, he planted the flag of the Explorers

Club, carefully he set up his camera, and then, as he prepared to shoot, his glance fell upon an object several feet away—an empty Kodak carton. Quietly, he repacked and stole away—and has stayed firmly on the beaten paths ever since.

As to politics, it never taints his lectures. He insists neither he nor his audiences are interested. "When you discuss politics," he says, "you are sure to offend." Even after his third trip to Russia, he refused to discuss politics. "I am a traveler," he explained at that time, "and not a student of political and economic questions. To me, Communism is merely one of the sights I went to see."

However, friends know that Holmes has his pet panacea for the ills of the world. He is violent about the gold standard, insisting that it alone can make all the world prosperous. Occasionally, when the mood is on him, and against his better judgment, he will inject propaganda in favor of the gold standard into an otherwise timid travelogue.

When he is feeling mellow, Holmes will confess that once in the past he permitted politics to intrude upon his sterile chitchat. It was two decades ago, when he jousted with Prohibition. While not a dedicated drinking man, Holmes has been on a friendly basis with firewater since the age of sixteen. In the ensuing years, he has regularly, every dusk before dinner, mixed himself one or two highballs. Only once did he try more than two, and the results were disastrous. "Any man who drinks three will drink three hundred," he now says righteously. Holmes felt that Prohibition was an insult to civilized living. As a consequence of this belief, his audiences during the days of the Eighteenth Amendment were often startled to hear Holmes extol the virtues of open drinking, in the middle of a placid discourse on Oberammergau or Lapland. "Sometimes an indignant female would return her tickets to the rest of my series," he says, "but there were others, more intelligent, to take her place."

This independent attitude in Holmes was solely the product of his personal success. Born in January, 1870, of a financially secure, completely cosmopolitan Chicago family, he was able to be independent from his earliest days. His father, an employee in the Third National Bank, distinguished himself largely by lending George Pullman enough cash to transform his old day coaches into the first Pullman Palace Sleeping Cars, and by refusing a half interest in the business in exchange for his help. Even to this day, it makes Burton Holmes dizzy to think of the money he might have saved in charges for Pullman berths.

Holmes's interest in show business began at the age of nine when his grandmother, Ann W. Burton, took him to hear John L. Stoddard lecture on the Passion Play at Oberammergau. Young Holmes was never the same again. After brief visits to faraway Florida and California, he quit school and accompanied his grandmother on his first trip abroad. He was sixteen and wide-eyed. His grandmother, who had traveled with her wine-salesman husband to France and Egypt and down the Volga in the sixties, was the perfect guide. But this journey through Europe was eclipsed, four years later, by a more important pilgrimage with his grandmother to Germany. The first day at his hotel in Munich, Holmes saw John L. Stoddard pass through the lobby reading a Baedeker. He was petrified. It was as if he had seen his Maker. Even now, over a half century later, when Holmes speaks about Stoddard, his voice carries a tinge of awe. For eighteen years of the later nineteenth century, Stoddard, with black-and-white slides and magnificent oratory, dominated the travel-lecture field. To audiences, young and old, he was the most romantic figure in America. Later, at Oberammergau, Holmes sat next to Stoddard through the fifteen acts of the Passion Play and they became friends.

When Holmes returned to the States, some months after Nellie Bly had made her own triumphal return to Brooklyn, he showed rare Kodak negatives of his travels to fellow members of the Chicago Camera Club. The members were impressed, and one suggested that these be mounted as slides and shown to the general public. "To take the edge off the silence, to keep the show moving," says Holmes, "I wrote an account of my journey and read it, as the stereopticon man changed slides." The show, which grossed the club $350, was Holmes's initial travelogue. However, he dates the beginning of his professional career from three years later, when he appeared under his own auspices with hand-colored slides.

After the Camera Club debut, Holmes did not go immediately into the travelogue field. He was not yet ready to appreciate its possibilities. Instead, he attempted to sell real estate, and failed. Then he worked for eight dollars a week as a photo supply clerk. In 1902, aching with wanderlust, he bullied his family into staking him to a five-month tour of Japan. On the boat he was thrilled to find John L. Stoddard, also bound for Japan. They became closer friends, even though they saw Nippon through different eyes. "The older man found Japan queer, quaint, comfortless, and almost repellent," Stoddard's son wrote years later. "To the younger man it was a fairyland." Stoddard invited Holmes to continue on around the world with him, but Holmes loved Japan and decided to remain.

When Holmes returned to Chicago, the World's Columbian Exposition of 1893 was in full swing. He spent months at the Jackson Park grounds, under Edison's new electric lights, listening to Lillian Russell sing, Susan B. Anthony speak, and watching Sandow perform feats of strength. With rising excitement, he observed Jim Brady eating, Anthony Comstock snorting at Little Egypt's hootchy-kootchy, and Alexander Dowie announcing himself as the Prophet Elijah III.

In the midst of this excitement came the depression of that year. Holmes's father suffered. "He hit the wheat pit at the wrong time, and I had to go out on my own," says Holmes. "The photo supply house offered me fifteen dollars a week to return. But I didn't want to work. The trip to Japan, the Oriental exhibits of the Exposition, were still on my mind. I thought of

Stoddard. I thought of the slides I'd had hand-colored in Tokyo. That was it, and it wasn't work. So I hired a hall and became a travel lecturer."

Copying society addresses from his mother's visiting list, and additional addresses from *The Blue Book,* Holmes mailed two thousand invitations in the form of Japanese poem-cards. Recipients were invited to two illustrated lectures, at $1.50 each, on "Japan—the Country and the Cities." Both performances were sellouts. Holmes grossed $700.

For four years Holmes continued his fight to win a steady following, but with only erratic success. Then, in 1897, when he stood at the brink of defeat, two events occurred to change his life. First, John L. Stoddard retired from the travel-lecture field and threw the platforms of the nation open to a successor. Second, Holmes supplemented colored slides with a new method of illustrating his talks. As his circular announced, "There will be presented for the first time in connection with a course of travel lectures a series of pictures to which a modern miracle has added the illusion of life itself—the reproduction of recorded motion."

Armed with his jumpy movies—scenes of the Omaha fire department, a police parade in Chicago, Italians eating spaghetti, each reel running twenty-five seconds, with a four-minute wait between reels—Burton Holmes invaded the Stoddard strongholds in the East. Stoddard came to hear him and observe the newfangled movies. Like Marshal Foch who regarded the airplane as "an impractical toy," Stoddard saw no future in the motion picture. Nevertheless, he gave young Holmes a hand by insisting that Augustin Daly lease his Manhattan theater to the newcomer. This done, Stoddard retired to the Austrian Tyrol, and Holmes went on to absorb Stoddard's audiences in Boston and Philadelphia and to win new followers of his own throughout the nation.

His success assured, Holmes began to gather material with a vigor that was to make him one of history's most indefatigable travelers. In 1900, at the Paris Exposition, sitting in a restaurant built like a Russian train, drinking vodka while a colored panorama of Siberia rolled past his window, he succumbed to this unique advertising of the new Trans-Siberian railway and bought a ticket. The trip in 1901 was a nightmare. After ten days on the Trans-Siberian train, which banged along at eleven miles an hour, Holmes was dumped into a construction train for five days, and then spent twenty-seven days on steamers going down the Amur River. It took him forty-two and a half days to travel from Moscow to Vladivostok.

But during that tour, he had one great moment. He saw Count Leo Tolstoi at Yasnaya Polyana, the author's country estate near Tula. At a dinner in Moscow, Holmes met Albert J. Beveridge, the handsome senator from Indiana. Beveridge had a letter of introduction to Tolstoi and invited Holmes and his enormous 60-mm movie camera to come along. Arriving in a four-horse landau, the Americans were surprised to find Tolstoi's house dilapidated. Then, they were kept waiting two hours. At last, the seventy-three-year-old, white-bearded Tolstoi, nine years away from his lonely death in a railway depot, appeared. He was attired in a mujik costume. He invited his visitors to breakfast, then conversed in fluent English. "He had only a slight accent, and he spoke with the cadence of Sir Henry Irving," Holmes recalls.

Of the entire morning's conversation, Holmes remembers clearly only one remark. That was when Tolstoi harangued, "There should be no law. No man should have the right to judge or condemn another. Absolute freedom of the individual is the only thing that can redeem the world. Christ was a great teacher, nothing more!" As Tolstoi continued to speak, Holmes quietly set up his movie camera. Tolstoi had never seen one before. He posed stiffly, as for a daguerreotype. When he thought that it was over, and resumed his talking, Holmes began actual shooting. This priceless film never reached the screen. Senator Beveridge was then a presidential possibility. His managers feared that this film of Beveridge with a Russian radical might be used by his opponents. The film was taken from Holmes and destroyed. Later, when he was not even nominated for the presidency, Beveridge wrote an apology to Holmes, "for this destruction of so valuable a living record of the grand old Russian."

In 1934, at a cost of ten dollars a day, Holmes spent twenty-one days in modern Soviet Russia. He loved the ballet, the omelets, the Russian rule against tipping, and the lack of holdups. He went twice to see the embalmed Lenin, fascinated by the sight of "his head resting on a red pillow like that of a tired man asleep."

Although Holmes's name had already appeared on eighteen travel volumes, this last Russian trip inspired him to write his first and only original book. The earlier eighteen volumes, all heavily illustrated, were offered as a set, of which over forty thousand were sold. However, they were not "written," but were actually a collection of lectures delivered orally by Holmes. The one book that he wrote as a book, *The Traveler's Russia,* published in 1934 by G.P. Putnam's Sons, was a failure. Holmes has bought the remainders and passes them out to guests with a variety of inscriptions. In a serious mood he will inscribe, "To travel is to possess the world." In a frivolous mood, he will write "With love from Tovarich Burtonovich Holmeski."

In the five decades past, Holmes has kept himself occupied with a wide variety of pleasures, such as attending Queen Victoria's Golden Jubilee in London, chatting with Admiral Dewey in Hong Kong, driving the first automobile seen in Denmark, and photographing a mighty eruption of Vesuvius.

In 1918, wearing a war correspondent's uniform, he shot army scenes on the Western Front and his films surpassed those of the poorly organized newsreel cameramen. In 1923, flying for the first time, he had his most dangerous experience, when his plane almost crashed between Toulouse and Rabat. Later, in

Berlin, he found his dollar worth ten million marks, and in Africa he interviewed Emperor Haile Selassie in French, and, closer to home, he flew 20,000 miles over Central and South America.

Burton Holmes enjoys company on his trips. By coincidence, they are often celebrities. Holmes traveled through Austria with Maria Jeritza, through Greece with E.F. Benson, through the Philippines with Dr. Victor Heiser. He covered World War I with Harry Franck, wandered about Japan with Lafcadio Hearn's son, crossed Ethiopia with the Duke of Gloucester. He saw Hollywood with Mary Pickford, Red Square with Alma Gluck, and the Andes with John McCutcheon.

Of the hundreds of travelogues that Holmes has delivered, the most popular was "The Panama Canal." He offered this in 1912, when the "big ditch" was under construction, and news-hungry citizens flocked to hear him. Among less timely subjects, his most popular was the standard masterpiece on Oberammergau, followed closely by his illustrated lectures on the "Frivolities of Paris," the "Canals of Venice," the "Countryside of England" and, more currently, "Adventures in Mexico." Burton Holmes admits that his greatest failure was an elaborate travelogue on Siam, even though it seemed to have everything except Anna and the King thereof. Other failures included travelogues on India, Burma, Ethiopia, and—curiously—exotic Bali. The only two domestic subjects to fizzle were "Down in Dixie" in 1915 and "The Century of Progress Exposition" in 1932.

All in all, the success of Holmes's subjects has been so consistently high that he has never suffered seriously from competition. One rival died, another retired eight years ago. "I'm the lone survivor of the magic-lantern boys," says Holmes. Of the younger crowd, Holmes thought that Richard Halliburton might become his successor. "He deserved to carry the banner," says Holmes. "He was good-looking, with a fine classical background, intelligent, interesting, and he really did those darn-fool stunts." Halliburton, who had climbed the Matterhorn, swum the Hellespont, followed the Cortés train through Mexico, lectured with slides. "I told him to throw away the slides," says Holmes. "He was better without them, his speech was so colorful." When Halliburton died attempting to sail a Chinese junk across the Pacific, Holmes decided to present an illustrated lecture on "The Romantic Adventures of Richard Halliburton." He used his own movies but, in the accompanying talk, Halliburton's written text. "It was a crashing failure," sighs Holmes. "His millions of fans did not want to hear me, and my fans did not want to know about him."

For a while, Hollywood appeared to be the travelogue's greatest threat. Holmes defeated this menace by marriage with the studios. He signed a contract with Paramount, made fifty-two travel shorts each year, between 1915 and 1921. Then, with the advent of talking pictures, Holmes joined Metro-Goldwyn-Mayer and made a series of travelogues, released in English, French, Italian, Spanish. In 1933, he made his debut in radio, and in 1944 made his first appearance on television.

Today, safe in the knowledge that he is an institution, Holmes spends more and more time in his rambling, plantation-style, wooden home, called "Topside," located on a hill a mile above crowded Hollywood Boulevard. This dozen-roomed brown house, once a riding club for silent day film stars, and owned for six years by Francis X. Bushman (who gave it Hollywood's first swimming pool, where Holmes now permits neighborhood children to splash), was purchased by Holmes in 1930. "I had that M-G-M contract," he says, "and it earned me a couple of hundred thousand dollars. Well, everyone with a studio contract immediately gets himself a big car, a big house, and a small blonde. I acquired the car, the house, but kept the blonde a mental acquisition." For years, Holmes also owned a Manhattan duplex decorated with costly Japanese and Buddhist treasures, which he called "Nirvana." Before Pearl Harbor, Holmes sold the duplex, with its two-million-dollar collection of furnishings, to Robert Ripley, the cartoonist and oddity hunter.

Now, in his rare moments of leisure, Holmes likes to sit on the veranda of his Hollywood home and chat with his wife. Before he met her, he had been involved in one public romance. Gossips, everywhere, insisted that he might marry the fabulous Elsie de Wolfe, actress, millionaire decorator, friend of Oscar Wilde and Sarah Bernhardt, who later became Lady Mendl. Once, in Denver, Holmes recalls, a reporter asked him if he was engaged to Elsie de Wolfe. Holmes replied, curtly, No. That afternoon a banner headline proclaimed: BURTON HOLMES REFUSES TO MARRY ELSIE DE WOLFE!

Shortly afterward, during a photographic excursion, Holmes met Margaret Oliver who, suffering from deafness, had taken up still photography as an avocation. In 1914, following a moonlight proposal on a steamer's deck, he married Miss Oliver in New York City's St. Stephen's Episcopal Church, and took her to prosaic Atlantic City for the first few days of their honeymoon, then immediately embarked on a long trip abroad.

When his wife is out shopping, Holmes will stroll about his estate, study his fifty-four towering palm trees, return to the veranda for a highball, thumb through the *National Geographic,* play with his cats, or pick up a language textbook. He is on speaking terms with eight languages, including some of the Scandinavian, and is eager to learn more. He never reads travel books. "As Pierre Loti once remarked, 'I don't read. It might ruin my style,'" he explains.

He likes visitors, and he will startle them with allusions to his earlier contemporaries. "This lawn part reminds me of the one at which I met Emperor Meiji," he will say. Meiji, grandfather of Hirohito, opened Japan to Commodore Perry. When visitors ask for his travel advice, Holmes invariably tells them to see the Americas first. "Why go to Mont St. Michel?" he asks. "Have you seen Monticello?"

But when alone with his wife and co-workers on the veranda,

and the pressure of the new season is weeks away, he will loosen his blue dressing gown, inhale, then stare reflectively out over the sun-bathed city below.

"You know, this is the best," he will say softly, "looking down on this Los Angeles. It is heaven. I could sit here the rest of my life." Then, suddenly, he will add, "There is so much else to see and do. If only I could have another threescore years upon this planet. If only I could know the good earth better than I do."

———

Note: Irving Wallace (1916-1990) wrote this article on the occasion of Burton Holmes's 77th birthday. It was originally printed in *The Saturday Evening Post* May 10, 1947. Holmes retired the following year from presenting his travelogues in person. He died in 1958 at age 88. His autobiography, *The World is Mine,* was published in 1953.

Reprinted by permission of Mrs. Sylvia Wallace.

BURTON HOLMES

By Arthur M. Schlesinger, jr.

B urton Holmes!—forgotten today, but such a familiar name in America in the first half of the 20th century, a name then almost synonymous with dreams of foreign travel. In the era before television brought the big world into the households of America, it was Burton Holmes who brought the world to millions of Americans in crowded lecture halls, and did so indefatigably for 60 years. I still remember going with my mother in the 1920s to Symphony Hall in Boston, watching the brisk, compact man with a Vandyke beard show his films of Venice or Bali or Kyoto and describe foreign lands in engaging and affectionate commentary.

Burton Holmes invented the word "travelogue" in 1904. He embodied it for the rest of his life. He was born in Chicago in 1870 and made his first trip abroad at the age of 16. Taking a camera along on his second trip, he mounted his black-and-white negatives on slides and showed them to friends in the Chicago Camera Club. "To keep the show moving," he said later, "I wrote an account of my journey and read it, as the stereopticon man changed slides." He had discovered his métier. Soon he had his slides hand-colored and was in business as a professional lecturer. In time, as technology developed, slides gave way to moving pictures.

Holmes was a tireless traveler, forever ebullient and optimistic, uninterested in politics and poverty and the darker side of life, in love with beautiful scenery, historic monuments, picturesque customs, and challenging trips. He was there at the Athens Olympics in 1896, at the opening of the Trans-Siberian railway, at the Passion Play in Oberammergau. His popular lectures had such titles as "The Magic of Mexico," "The Canals of Venice," "The Glories and Frivolities of Paris." His illustrated travel books enthralled thousands of American families. He also filmed a series of travelogues—silent pictures for Paramount, talkies for Metro-Goldwyn-Mayer.

He wanted his fellow countrymen to rejoice in the wonders of the great globe. "I'm a Cook's tourist," he said, referring to the famous tours conducted by Thomas Cook and Sons, "reporting how pleasant it is in such and such a place." He knew that the world was less than perfect, but he thought the worst sufficiently documented, and his mission, as he saw it, was to bring people the best. Reflecting at the end of the Second World War on the mood of returning veterans, he said, "The atrocities and miseries will be difficult to forget. I know I can't give my Beautiful Italy lecture next session to men who know Italy only as a pigsty . . . One day these boys will forget and come to my lectures not to hoot but to relive the better moments and enjoy themselves."

When he retired in 1951, Burton Holmes had delivered over 8,000 lectures. By the time he died in 1958, television had taken over the job he had discharged so ardently for more than half a century. He taught generations of Americans about the great world beyond the seas. His books are still readable today and show new generations how their grandparents learned about a world that has since passed away but remains a fragrant memory.

THE WORLD 100 YEARS AGO

By Dr. Fred Israel

The generation that lived 100 years ago was the first to leave behind a comprehensive visual record. It was the camera that made this possible. The great photographers of the 1860s and 1870s took their unwieldy equipment to once-unimaginable places—from the backstreets of London to the homesteads of the American frontier; from tribal Africa to the temples of Japan. They photographed almost the entire world.

Burton Holmes (1870-1958) ranks among the pioneers who popularized photojournalism. He had an insatiable curiosity. "There was for me the fascination of magic in photography," Holmes wrote. "The word Kodak had not yet been coined. You could not press the button and let someone else do the rest. You had to do it all yourself and know what you were doing." Holmes combined his love of photography with a passion for travel. It didn't really matter where—only that it be exciting.

"Shut your eyes, tight!" said Holmes. "Imagine the sands of the Sahara, the temples of Japan, the beach at Waikiki, the fjords of Norway, the vastness of Panama, the great gates of Peking." It was this type of visual imagination that made Burton Holmes America's best known travel lecturer. By his 75th birthday, he had crossed the Atlantic Ocean 30 times and the Pacific 20, and he had gone around the world on six occasions. Variety magazine estimated that in his five-decade career, Holmes had delivered more than 8,000 lectures describing almost every corner of the earth.

Burton Holmes was born in Chicago on January 8, 1870. His privileged background contributed to his lifelong fascination with travel. When he was 16, his maternal grandmother took him on a three-month European trip, about which he later wrote:

> I still recall our first meal ashore, the delicious English sole served at the Adelphi Hotel [Liverpool] . . . Edinburgh thrilled me, but Paris! I would gladly have travelled third class or on a bike or on foot. Paris at last! I knew my Paris in advance. Had I not studied the maps and plans? I knew I could find my way to Notre Dame and to the Invalides without asking anyone which way to go. (The Eiffel Tower had not yet been built.) From a bus-top, I surveyed the boulevards—recognizing all the famous sights. Then for a panoramic survey of the city, I climbed the towers of Notre Dame, then the Tour St. Jacques, the Bastille Column, and finally the Arc De Triomphe, all in one long day. That evening, I was in Montmartre, where as yet there stood no great domed church of the Sacre Coeur. But at the base of the famous hill were the red windmill wings of the Moulin Rouge revolving in all their majesty. My French—school French—was pretty bad but it sufficed. Paris was the springtime of my life!

Holmes never lost his passion for travel nor his passion for capturing his observations on film. He has left us with a unique and remarkable record that helps us to visualize the world many decades ago.

Lecturing became Holmes's profession. In 1892-93 he toured Japan. He discovered that "it was my native land in some previous incarnation—and the most beautiful land I have known." Holmes had the idea of giving an illustrated lecture about Japan to an affluent Chicago audience:

> I had brought home a large number of Japanese cards such as
> are used in Japan for sending poems or New Year's greetings.
> They were about two inches by fourteen inches long. I had the
> idea that they would, by their odd shape, attract instant notice.
> So I had envelopes made for them, employing a Japanese artist
> to make a design.

Holmes sent about 2,000 invitations to the socially prominent
whose addresses he took from the *Blue Book*. He "invited" them
to two illustrated lectures at $1.50 each on "Japan—the Country
and the Cities." ($1.50 was a high sum for the 1890s considering
that the average worker earned about $1 per day.) Both perfor-
mances sold out.

Burton Holmes's "Travelogues" (he began using the term in
1904) rapidly became part of American upper class societal life.
Holmes engaged the best theater or concert hall for a week at a
time. His appearance was an annual event at Carnegie Hall in
New York, Symphony Hall in Boston, and Orchestra Hall in
Chicago. His uncanny instinct for exciting programs invariably
received rave reviews. Once he explained how he selected his
photographic subjects:

> If I am walking through Brussels and see a dog cart or some
> other unimportant thing that is interesting enough for me to
> watch it, I am totally certain others would be interested in seeing
> a photograph of it.

A conservative man, Holmes avoided political upheavals,
economic exploitation, and social conflicts in his travelogues.
"When you discuss politics," he said, "you are sure to offend."
Holmes focused on people, places, and customs. He offered his
audience a world which was unfailingly tranquil and beautiful.

In 1897, Holmes introduced motion picture segments into his
programs. ("Neapolitans Eating Spaghetti" was his first film
clip.) His engaging personality contributed to his success. His

crisp narrative was delivered in a pleasant and cultured tone. He always wore formal dress with striped pants before an audience. Holmes took pride in creating an atmosphere so that his listeners could imagine the "Magic of Mexico" or the "Frivolities of Paris." "My first ambition was to be a magician," he said. "And, I never departed from creating illusions. I have tried to create the illusion that we are going on a journey. By projecting the views, I tried to create the illusion we are looking through 'the window of travel' upon shifting scenes." Holmes's travelogues were immensely successful financially—and Holmes became one of history's most indefatigable travelers.

Holmes's lectures took place during the winter months between the 1890s and his retirement in the early 1950s. In between, he traveled—he crossed Morocco on horseback from oasis to oasis (1894); he was in the Philippines during the 1899 insurrection; in 1901, he traversed the Russian Empire, going from Moscow to Vladivostok in 43 days. He visited Yellowstone National Park (1896) before it had been fully mapped. He was always on the move, traveling to: Venice (1896); London (1897); Hawaii (1898); The Philippines (1899); Paris (1900); Russia, China, and Korea (1901-02); Madeira, Lisbon, Denmark, and Sweden (1902); Arizona, California, and Alaska (1903); Switzerland (1904); Russia and Japan (1905); Italy, Greece, Egypt, and Hong Kong (1906); Paris, Vienna, and Germany (1907); Japan (1908); Norway (1909); Germany and Austria (1910); Brazil, Argentina, and Peru (1911); Havana and Panama (1912); India and Burma (1913); the British Isles (1914); San Francisco (1915); Canada (1916); Australia and New Zealand (1917); Belgium and Germany (1919); Turkey and the Near East (1920); England (1921); China (1922); North Africa (1923); Italy (1924); Ceylon (1925); Holland (1926); France (1927); Spain (1928); London (1929); Ethiopia (1930); California (1931); Java (1932); Chicago (1933); the Soviet Union (1934); Normandy and Brittany (1935); South America (1936); South Africa (1937); Germany (1938).

Holmes's black and white photographs have extraordinary clarity. His sharp eye for the unusual ranks him as a truly outstanding photographer and chronicler of the world.

Holmes's lectures on the Panama Canal were his most popular—cities added extra sessions. For Holmes though, his favorite presentation was always Paris—"no city charms and fascinates us like the city by the Seine." He found Athens in the morning to be the most beautiful scene in the world—"with its pearl lights and purple-blue shadows and the Acropolis rising in mystic grandeur." Above all though, Japan remained his favorite land—"one can peel away layer after layer of the serene contentment which we mistake for expressionlessness and find new beauties and surprises beneath each." And Kyoto, once the capital, was the place he wanted most to revisit—and revisit. Holmes never completed a travelogue of New York City—"I am saving the biggest thing in the world for the last." At the time of his death in 1958 at age 88, Holmes had visited most of the world. He repeatedly told interviewers that he had lived an exciting and fulfilling life because he had accomplished his goal—to travel.

In a time before television, Burton Holmes was for many people "The Travelogue Man." He brought the glamour and excitement of foreign lands to Americans unable to go themselves. His successful career spanned the years from the Spanish-American War in 1898 to the Cold War of the 1950s—a period when Americans were increasingly curious about distant places and peoples. During this time period, travel was confined to a comparative handful of the privileged. Holmes published travelogues explaining foreign cultures and customs to the masses.

In this series of splendid travel accounts, Holmes unfolds before our eyes the beauties of foreign lands as they appeared almost a century ago. These volumes contain hundreds of photographs taken by Holmes. Through his narratives and illustrations we are transported in spirit to the most interesting countries and cities of the world.

PARIS

The Eiffel Tower, Notre Dame, the Arc de Triomphe, and all the other historic monuments that Burton Holmes describes can be seen in so many photographs and paintings that they can fade behind familiarity. Yet, it takes only a momentary change—a figure in the photograph, a personal story in his essay—to rescue such well-known sights from the postcard views. Holmes's descriptions and his sharp illustrations give us his view of Paris. Seen this way, our affection for this city can only increase.

Burton Holmes first traveled to Paris in 1886 when he was 16. He returned many times. To Holmes, Paris was the most beautiful city in the world. "With every recurring visit," he wrote, "I find that I gaze on it with a sense of novelty, an interest and a pleasure for which I can find no expression in words." Through his text and photographs, Holmes captures both the atmosphere and temperament of what he called "the capital of the world."

This Paris travelogue describes the city between 1890 and 1910, a period known as the Belle Epoque. Paris was then the center of European culture. Probably never before in history had so many innovative and creative people lived in one city. In art there was Claude Monet (1840-1926); Auguste Renoir (1841-1919); Paul Cézanne (1839-1906); Edgar Degas (1834-1917); Paul Gauguin (1848-1903) and Pablo Picasso (1881-1973). In music, Claude Debussy (1862-1916) must rank as the greatest of his day. His basic aim was to create sheer unadulterated sensuous pleasure through the most delicately developed musical tones. His opera *Pellar et Melisande* is a landmark in the history of opera.

The Belle Epoque years saw an art form new to western Europe appear in Paris. It was ballet, particularly the Ballet Russe under the direction of Sergei Diaghilev. Ballet had been performed in Paris before but usually as part of an opera. Now it became an art form in its own right—and an enormously popular one. This was its "Golden Age" dominated by such dancers as Nijinsky and Pavlova. Scores written by Igor Stravinsky for *Rite of Spring* and *Firebird* still rank as the most innovative music composed for ballet. Most of those involved in ballet during the Belle Epoque years were not French, but it was in Paris that this new art form was perfected. It was Paris that introduced ballet to the rest of the western world.

In sculpture, Auguste Rodin (1840-1917) towers above all others. His daring vision and originality made him world famous. Rodin lived in the Hotel Biron on the left bank of the Seine River. Today, it is the Musée Rodin. Probably his best known work is *The Thinker,* a great bronze figure which now stands in front of the Panthéon.

It is Paris of the Belle Epoque that Holmes describes in this travelogue. He describes a city that was made to be enjoyed, a city that boasted the best theaters and the best restaurants as well as the finest museums and bookshops. He describes a city of buildings with six, seven, and eight stories, constructed from cream-colored limestone and decorated with black wrought iron. He includes photographs of the picturesque roofs of the city, capturing their charm.

Today, tens of thousands of tourists descend on Paris each day. In the years 1890-1910, however, very few could afford the luxury of being a tourist in Paris. Many learned about the city through this Burton Holmes travelogue. The Paris that Holmes toured abounded with curiosities to be discovered at almost every turn. We follow Holmes along the Grand Boulevards and through the Bohemian Latin Quarter. We sit with Holmes in elegant restaurants and also share with him delight with a Left Bank bistro. Through this book, Holmes conveys the magnificence of the greatest city in Europe at the dawn of the 20th century.

P ARIS

THERE is no place in all the world like Paris. No city charms
and fascinates us like the city by the Seine. None of the
world's great capitals is so truly the capital of the great world.

Whoever you may be, whatever things attract you, you will
be at home in Paris; you will find there the very thing you seek —
Paris is all things to all men.

The artist finds a Paris that is one great studio, from Montmartre all the way to Montparnasse. The student finds a Paris that
is one vast university, from the Sorbonne to the Bibliothèque Ste.
Geneviève. The pleasure-seeker finds a Paris that is one wide

world of pleasure, from the Moulin Rouge to Maxim's. The Bohemian finds a Paris that is all Bohemia, from the Quartier Latin to the Outer Boulevards. The votary of fashion finds a Paris that is an exquisite exhibition of finery from the Rue de la Paix to Longchamps, and a broad "peacock alley" from the Hotel Ritz to Paillard's in the Pré Catelan. The theater-goer finds a Paris that is all a stage, and on that stage he finds the world's most noted stages.

The lover of the horse finds a Paris rich in the finest race-tracks in the world, from Auteuil to Maisons-Laffitte. The motorist finds a Paris that is the native city of the motor-car and the home of the automobile industry. The sight-seer finds a Paris that is a world of sights from the grim Cabaret du Néant to the marble halls of the Louvre where the Venus de Milo is enshrined. The scholar finds a Paris that is a volume of French History

THE GARE DE LYON

written in sculptured stone. The thinker finds a Paris that is the brain of Europe. In a word, Paris is everything to everybody; but above all, Paris is Paris, and whichever side of Paris pleases you, I hope that you may find a little of your Paris in this Travelogue.

AVENUE DE L'OPÉRA

The traveler finds the heart and center of his Paris at the Place de l'Opéra — where the full life-tide of the Grand Boulevards rolls past the grandest temple of music in the world. There are a hundred good hotels within a few squares of this famous focal point of Parisian existence. I shall not advise you in the choice of your hotel; so much depends upon what you mean to do, and the means you have for doing it; but I must urgently recommend that you pass your first leisure hour in Paris at the corner table of the *terrasse* of the Café de la Paix; the *terrasse* means that part of the sidewalk leased by the café from the municipality and covered by the closely set chairs and tables of the establishment. This corner is regarded by Boulevardiers as the very center of the world. It is a fact known and proved, that if you want to find a friend in Paris you have only to sit here at this corner long enough; he is sure to pass in time. No stranger can sit here for an hour without seeing some one whom he knows or used to know. Once, however, as I took my place here after an absence of some months, I was a trifle disappointed not to see at first glance some well-known face, but as I looked at the familiar news kiosk on the curb, at which I have always bought my "Figaro" to read while sipping the delicious chocolate and

CAFÉ DE LA PAIX

eating the good *brioche* which always make up my "little breakfast" when in Paris, there, displayed among the periodicals was the inevitable well-known face — there in the upper left-hand corner — the face of our American tenor George Hamlin, on the front page of the latest issue of the "Musical Courier." The next time that I came to the Café de la Paix, two young Americans, just arrived for the first

A NEWS KIOSK

time in Paris, greet me sadly — because my appearance makes them lose a bet. They have wagered with a more experienced traveler that they could sit at the café for an hour without meeting an acquaintance, and that is why they are not glad to see me.

Another time — an incident even more striking — just arrived from Ceylon, via Suez and Marseilles, I sit me down to enjoy my afternoon *apéritif* at my accustomed tiny table on that well-trodden sidewalk; two ladies and a gentleman, Americans, simultaneously take the table next to mine. The three look at me and then at one another — smile in amazement, and one of them exclaims, ."Well, Mr.

"CAOUTCHOUC"

Holmes, this is *too* good. The first thing we do in Paris is to come here just to test the truth of what you said in your lecture about being sure to meet some one you know at the Café de la Paix, and whom do we see but *you!*" A better name for this establishment would not be hard to invent, for it is anything but

PLACE DE

a "Café of Peace." It should be called the *Cabaret de Caoutchouc,* and *caoutchouc* is the French word that stands for "rubber." At this corner everything and everybody stands for "rubber" and "to rubber"; it is the most elastic corner in all Paris. The neck of the true Parisian never loses its elasticity, his eye its elasticity of gaze. In Paris it is not considered rude to stare. On the contrary, what would be the use of all the pretty hats and gowns and high-heeled shoes and dainty hosiery if men were not gallant enough to pay attention to the exquisite display? So while in Paris let us do as the Parisians do, and standing, or sitting, if you please, at the Café de la Paix, let us also "rubber" to our heart's content at the marvelous array of interesting humanity that surges past.

The Grand Opera House of Paris is styled officially the National Academy of Music. It is the largest theater building

L'OPÉRA

in the world, although its auditorium seats only about two thousand persons, six hundred less than Carnegie Hall in New York, and less than half as many as the Chicago Auditorium. It cost nearly ten million dollars. It has been in almost constant use since 1874, summer as well as winter, enjoying always generous patronage, no matter what operas or artists are announced. It receives a subsidy of six hundred thousand francs a year, and being a national enterprise, all operas must be sung in the French language. We managed to go on behind the scenes one night,

during a presenta-
tion of Gounod's
ever-fascinating
Faust; not know-
ing any one high in
authority we ar-
ranged with some
scene shifters to
smuggle us in
through the stage
door. They did
it; but we had to

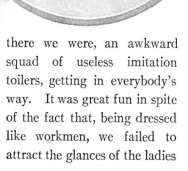

go as scene shifters, wearing
the soiled uniforms of ab-
sent stage hands, blue
overalls and blouses and
Frenchy little caps. And

there we were, an awkward
squad of useless imitation
toilers, getting in everybody's
way. It was great fun in spite
of the fact that, being dressed
like workmen, we failed to
attract the glances of the ladies

GARNIER, ARCHITECT OF THE OPERA

of the ballet. After we had helped pull ropes and shift scenes we had time, while Faust and Marguerite were singing the sweetest love music ever written, to climb aloft into the flies up through eight tiers of galleries where ropes and drops and backgrounds hang — and to go down into the cavernous cellars, four stories underground, and there we looked down through the trap-door in the pavement and saw the black waters of a river, a subterranean river that loses itself in the

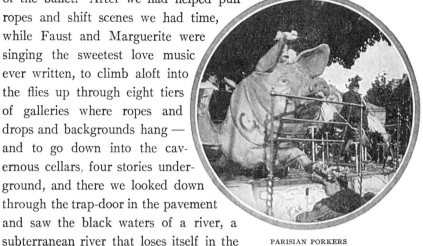

PARISIAN PORKERS

THE "RED MILL" IN THE WHITE PLACE

soil underneath this part of Paris. Sometimes that river rises and floods out the cellars, in spite of all the pumps that are kept always ready for a like emergency. That stream comes down from Montmartre, the hill now crowned by the new Basilica of the Sacred Heart. All this part of town was once a swamp. This fact is recalled by the name of one of the neighboring streets, the Rue de la Chaussée d'Antin, so called because the causeway or *chaussée* over the swamp at this point was paved at the expense of the

MAIDENS OF MONT-
MARTRE

Marquis of Antin about two hundred years ago.

We know, of course, that the Boulevards of modern Paris take their name from the Bulwarks of the medieval city. Those old fortifications were leveled in the reign of Louis XIV: broad avenues were laid out where the walls had stood and on the site of one of the many old-time gates, called the Porte St. Denis, a tri-

BASILICA OF THE SACRED HEART

umphal arch was erected in 1673 in honor of the victories of the
Grand Monarque in Holland and in Germany.   Through the old
Porte St. Denis the French Kings used to make their entries into
Paris after coronation and their exits from the city after death,
when they were carried in solemn state to the suburban Abbey of
St. Denis, mausoleum of the Kings of France for the last thirteen

THE BOURSE

hundred years.   But it would take us too long to pick up and
unravel all of those threads of history and romance that form
dense tangles at every crossing of the old Paris streets; so, break-
ing through a thousand strands of interest we find ourselves at
the eastern end of the Grand Boulevards in the Place de la Bastille.   This square is clogged with historical associations; but
all the strands of the glorious tangle lead to the central fact that
here the people of Paris captured and tore down that famous
prison that was the symbol of monarchical misrule.

Here the French Revolution was born on July 14, 1789.
The column, called the July Column, commemorates the Revolu-

tion of 1830, which in those three famous July days
overthrew the Bourbon king, Charles X and paved
the way for the accession of Louis Philippe.   And
he in turn was overthrown in 1848, when this same
square was bathed again in blood, and
Louis Philippe's throne was burned here
on the same spot where sleep the victims of the July Revolution that had
set him on that throne.   Then came
the awful days of 1871 when the
insurgents of the Commune made
their last stand behind the barricades here in the Place de la Bastille.
Of the Bastille itself nothing remains;
but the place where it stood is outlined
by easily traced lines of paving-stones —
perhaps the very paving-stones that were

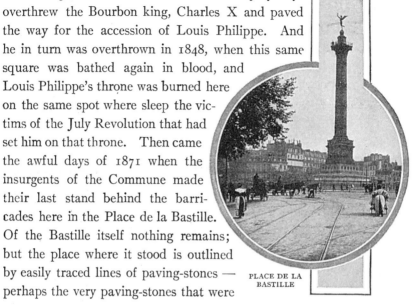

PLACE DE LA
BASTILLE

PORTE ST. DENIS

thrown up to form the barricades of 1871. The Bastille was originally one of the fortified city gates of Paris. It was left intact when
the walls were demolished and became famous, or infamous, as
the prison to which political offenders were committed and to
which any favorite of the King could send his innocent enemies,
provided he had secured one of those blank warrants, called
lettres-de-cachet, which were often given freely as rewards to those
who had served royalty or pandered to its vices.

Thus the Bastille became in popular estimation the symbol of
that despotism under which the French people had been reduced
almost to starvation. Therefore the first cry of the revolutionary mob, aroused at last by the belief that the populous
quarters near the ancient fortress-gate were to be bombarded
by its cannon, was "Down with the Bastille!" — and that
shout, like the shout that rose around the walls of Jericho, did
result in bringing down those walls. The Bastille was taken
in a day, and within a few days demolished. Its stones now
form the arches of the Pont de la Concorde, the bridge that
leads from the Place de la Concorde to the Chamber of Deputies.

It is affirmed
that the Bastille
was in fact merely
a scape-goat for
the fury of the
populace; that it
was the prison
rather of the ene-
mies of the people,
where the lawless
nobles were pun-
ished for their
crimes. When it
was taken the mob
found no patriot

THE PAVING STONES THAT TELL WHERE THE BASTILLE
STOOD

martyrs there: only seven prisoners were discovered in its sup-
posedly crowded dungeons, and of them four were forgers — common criminals awaiting trial. Even Marat, who cannot be
accused of favoring the royal cause, declared that the people
had no right to hold the Bastille in abhorrence — but it had

WAXEN BEAUTIES

become the symbol of what the people rightly did abhor, and
of it they left not one stone upon another.

Fashion has never favored this part of Paris. We are near
the populous quarters — St. Antoine, still turbulent with that
spirit that gives life to insurrections and to revolutions — and
Père Lachaise, with its ever-increasing, never-decreasing popula-
tion of Parisian dead. Fashion makes its headquarters in another
famous square where stands another famous monument of metal
— the bronze column that commemorates the victories of Napoleon over the Austrians and Russians — especially the victory
of Austerlitz. The Vendôme Column, cast from captured cannon,

was set up in 1806. It is a metal paraphrase of the Trajan Column which lifts its marble shaft, adorned with its spiral band of sculptured war-scenes in a forum of old Rome. And like Trajan's monument, the Vendôme Column has known more than one tenant on its top. St. Peter's effigy has supplanted that of Trajan there in Rome. Here in Paris, Napoleon's form was

not only removed—but melted down and re-cast. The Napoleonic metal is seen to-day in the form of Henry of Navarre, who sits astride his charger and like a member of some antiquated "traffic squad " tries to regu-late the flow of traffic over the old "New Bridge," the old "Pont Neuf." Under the Restoration a huge Bourbon fleur-de-lis flaunted itself like the flame of that enormous bronze candle in the Place Vendôme — and

like a candle flame, it was blown out by the breath of the July Rev-olution. Un-der Louis Philippe, the "Citizen King," a new but unimpres-sive Napoleon in modern dress perched for a

THE VENDÔME COLUMN

time there on the historic pinnacle, but finally — under Napoleon III — ceded its place to the nobler image of Bonaparte in classic garb that now looks down upon the fashionable hotels of this exclusive square. But even this latest tenant of the top has had its sensational vicissitudes. The entire column was pulled down by the Communists in 1871, and for a time lay like a colossal sewer-pipe, blocking one side of the spacious square of which it is to-day the glory and the ornament. The street that leads from the Place Vendôme to the Opéra is the cele-

THE SHOPPERS AND THE SHOW-GIRLS

brated Rue de la Paix, the street dear to the heart of the American woman and dearer to the purse of her indulgent husband. It's lots of fun to go out shopping with Americans in Paris, especially when with some one who really means to order several gowns. The fashionable dressmaking establishments make it pleasant for the men who trapse along; the women of course find pleasure in looking at the frocks; the men find even more in looking at the pretty living models or *mannequins* upon whose shapely forms the new frocks are displayed. These stately show-girls sweep into the apartment with the air of uncrowned Empresses, oblivious to the humble would-be purchasers of the finery which usually becomes the poor but pretty *mannequin* much better 'than it does the purse-proud customer. Mere man, of course, will be inclined to pity the poor girls — condemned to strut all day in costly finery that becomes them so well, yet never can become their own. But apparently no pangs of

JEANNE D'ARC

jealousy are felt, even by the less lovely demoiselle who takes my lady's measure so deftly and, as it seems, so carelessly. We mere men cannot understand how the gowns ever can be made to fit, when the specifications are so quickly taken and set down — but here we realize that we are getting beyond our depth and so we prudently withdraw, and, wandering along the Rue de Rivoli, pause to study the gilded habiliments of Jeanne d'Arc, whose equestrian statue stands in the Place Rivoli, and to wonder how her costume of bright steel was ever made to fit so perfectly. Here again is occasion for a long historical digression, but the noble story of the Maid of Orléans is too fine, too rich in beauty and inspiration, to be crowded in between a visit to the dressmaker and a ramble in the Rue de Rivoli. I hope some day to tell the picture-story of Jeanne d'Arc; no story could be more variously picturesque than the tale that begins in the pious calm of the village of

RUE DE RIVOLI

THE COMÉDIE FRANÇAISE

Domrémy and passing through the blood of battlefields and the splendor of royal courts ends at the stake amid the flames of sacrifice. Every point of Paris recalls a tragedy or drama. The history of Paris is one long series of connected plays, the most intensely dramatic that history has ever penned. No wonder that the French nation gives the world great actors, greater actresses, and plays that stir the emotions of humanity. In Paris we find the chief playhouse of the modern world, the oldest of great theaters, the home of the most nearly perfect acting that can be seen in all the world to-day. It is called both " Le Théâtre Français " and " La Comédie Française." It is the National

ALFRED DE MUSSET

Conservatory of Dramatic Art. It has given us such names
as Bernhardt, Bartet, Coquelin, Mounet-Sully, Got, Lambert,
and Le Bargy. It is the home of the oldest classics and of the
newest problem play — the one played with broad inspiration,
the other with inimitable finesse. Night
after night we may enjoy the work
of the best company of players
in the world; one night in the
antique tragedy of "Edipus
the King," the next in the
latest of the year's suc-
cesses, and the next in
some dainty and poetic
trifle from the pen of the
idol of an earlier Parisian
Bohemia, Alfred de Musset,
who died in 1857. A statue
of the tearful poet has been
placed recently at the corner of the
building; on the pedestal we read his
famous lines:

CAMILLE DESMOULINS

"*Rien ne nous rend si grands qu'une grande douleur —*
Les plus désespérés sont les chants les plus beaux —
Et j'en sais d'immortels qui sont de pures sanglots,"

which I have ventured roughly to translate:

"Nothing can make us greater than a great, great grief —
The sweetest songs are those of hopelessness —
And I know some immortal ones that are pure sobs of deep
    distress."

But Alfred de Musset had a gay time while he lived, and his sor-
rows are not those on which a healthy-minded Anglo-Saxon can
waste much sympathy.

The statue of a man more after our own heart stands in the neighboring garden of the Palais Royal, where we see Camille Desmoulins in the very act of rising to harangue the excited crowd assembled there on July 12, 1789. Two days later the people took and tore down the old Bastille. His words fired the fuse of the French Revolution. In his impassioned speech he bade the

GARDEN OF THE PALAIS ROYAL

people assume a green cockade: the trees of this garden furnished the leaves that formed that badge of hope. Fitting indeed that the revolutionary fire should have spread from this Palais Royal which had been the scene of the scandalous orgies and excesses of the Regent's Court during early years of the reign of Louis XV.

Later the grandson of that Prince of Orleans, Philippe-Egalité, revived there the traditions of his house for costly debauchery, and in order to pay the piper had to increase his income by erecting and renting the buildings that now surround the garden. At one time the shops and cafés of the Palais Royal were the most popular in Paris, but fickle fashion has forsaken them for those

COURT OF HÔTEL DE VILLE

of the Rue de la Paix and of the Boulevards. The cheap table d'hôte is now served where not long ago the *gourmets* feasted; and cheap jewelry now sparkles flashily in windows where the finest and rarest gems once gleamed with ray serene.

The garden itself, where a band plays frequently, is the playground of the children of the neighborhood and the rendezvous of nurse-maids and soldiers and the refuge of long-haired idlers and sad-looking women, who come to dream away sad hours in the garden that was once the haunt of the gayest of the gay. Still gay enough — in fact, too gay for all save the most hardened admirers of the suggestive farces that delight the Paris public — are the plays acted with exquisite *verve* and *diablerie* by the clever players of the Théâtre du Palais Royal, which occupies one corner of the great quadrangle. So marvelously deft is the dramatic touch of the Gallic playwrights and players, and so wonderfully does the language lend itself both to *double entendre* and to a frank utterance of what would be unutterably vulgar in any other tongue, that even the most shocking things may be said and done on the Palais Royal stage without shocking the eminently respectable people who pack the house nightly, and roar themselves into convulsions over scenes that could never be presented on the English-speaking stage.

The Palace was burned by the Communists in 1871, as were many other famous buildings, including the Hôtel de Ville — the City Hall of Paris — which has since been splendidly restored. It is the finest purely modern pile in Paris: but it marks a site reeking with tragic memories. There in the Place de Grève was the old execution ground of earlier centuries. There Louis XI had an accused assassin torn to pieces by four horses; there Ravaillac, who murdered Henri IV, was literally cut to bits; there Damiens, who tried to kill Louis XV, had his guilty hand burned off before being subjected to tortures still more barbarous; there after the fall of the Bastille, its governor was de-

THE HÔTEL DE VILLE

capitated by the crowd; and to go back to earlier times, there the young King Philip, who reigned in the twelfth century, was killed by a fall from his horse — the accident caused by a pig running between the horse's legs. Since then it has not been lawful to allow four-legged pigs to wander about in Paris.

The Hôtel de Ville has been called the "Louvre of Robespierre," who during his brief, terrible régime made it the seat of his government of terror; and there, too, he met his downfall, and in the moment of defeat, feebly attempting sui-cide, merely shattered his jaw with a bullet instead of blowing out his brains. Had Robespierre gripped the pistol as coolly and as firmly as he gripped for a time the scepter of the Terror, the guillotine would have been robbed of its prey and the drama of French history would have lacked one of its most effective cli-maxes. From the upper windows of the Hôtel de Ville — or better still, from

THE TOWER OF ST. JACQUES

the top of the neighboring Tower of St. Jacques — all that is left
of a sixteenth-century Gothic church — a splendid bird's-eye panorama of Paris is revealed.   We look westward — down the Seine —
counting seven of the twenty-seven bridges that span the river between Charenton and Auteuil.   Counting the shorter bridges that
span the narrow   branches   of
the Seine   between

LOOKING TOWARD NOTRE DAME

the Latin   Quarter
and the islands   of St. Louis and
La Cité there are   seven more —
making a total of thirty-four fine bridges — all, with one or two
exceptions, either artistic or imposing.

A very interesting morning may be spent in cruising up and
down the Seine in the little river steamers — popularly known as
Bateaux Mouches—Fly Boats — which flit along the stream from
station to station discharging or receiving passengers at the little
floating landing-stages where very brief stops are made.   The
fare is only ten *centimes* — two cents in American money.   Each
passenger is supposed to purchase, while en route, a metal check,

THE BRIDGE OF AUTEUIL AND A SUBURBAN TRAIN

or *jeton*, and this he drops into the hand of the conductor of the "water omnibus" as he steps ashore at his destination. On Sundays and holidays the fare is doubled, and yet the number of passengers carried is quadrupled, for the Paris populace appreciates the advantages of these little river journeys up and down the beautiful, historic Seine. In fact, it is always a pleasure, even for one to whom Paris is familiar, to glide under one historic bridge after another, to gaze up at the beautiful façades of the Louvre and the Tuileries and other buildings in which history has been made — or in which famous art treasures are enshrined —

THE BRIDGE OF PASSY AND A
SUBWAY TRAIN

and to see lifting their ancient noble forms against the sky, the Towers of Notre Dame, la Tour St. Jacques, the domes of the Institute and of the Panthéon, all these famous shapes, apparently shifting their relative positions and forming new and ever-changing compositions as the *Bateaux Mouches* slip silently along the historic waterway that winds through the greatest and most wonderful of Continental cities.

Nowhere in the world can one enjoy, for so little expenditure of time and money, a more impressive moving panorama, historical, artistic, and rich in a charm that is not explicable to those who do not know Paris and love it, for it is the *charm of Paris,* — a charm that is indefinable, yet one from which we who do love Paris never can escape. The most famous of the many bridges under which we pass is the old Pont Neuf — the "New Bridge"

A STATION OF THE "METRO"

that is really older than any of the others. It was finished in 1604; it was to old Paris what the Boulevard near the Café de la Paix is to the Paris of to-day: it was the center of life and gayety, the place where

every one was sure to pass. The police used to say that if they watched three days in succession for any man they "wanted" and he did not pass, it was cer-

THE WOMAN CABBY

tain that he was either dead or departed. The Pont Neuf is a double bridge traversing the narrow western end of the island called l'Isle de la Cité and spanning both branches of the Seine. Below it, extending westward like the low prow of a ship of stone — the decks of which are deep-covered with a cargo of verdure — is one of my favorite little corners of "Quiet Paris" — a peaceful, pretty garden, the Jardin Henri IV. Few foreigners ever find their way down the steep steps

LA FEMME COCHÈRE

behind the famous statue of Henry of Navarre and into the cool, calm, triangular little park that bears his name, and which was at one time a separate island — a sand-spit called l'Isle des Treilles — joined to the larger island of La Cité when the foundations of the bridge were laid.   More familiar than the garden of Henri IV is the equestrian statue of that grand old King that dominates the

THE ISLAND OF LA CITÉ AND THE PONT NEUF

place where the Pont Neuf rests itself there in midstream.   The royal rider and the royal horse are made of the bronze that once incarnated the Imperial Napoleon on the Colonne Vendôme — the bronze that that same Napoleon had taken, in the form of cannon, from his enemies; and the original statue of Henri IV, which was set up here in 1635, was melted down in 1792 and recast in the form of revolutionary cannon.   The Revolution paved the way for the Dictator, who later on, as Emperor, was to take from the Austrians and Russians the gun metal that went into the making of the Napoleonic monument in the Place Vendôme, and of which a part has served in the restoration of the noble figure of great Henry of Navarre, presiding genius of the old Pont Neuf.

Along the lower *quais* that surround the Garden of Henri IV and stretch along under the bridges are the haunts of many curious types of poor Parisians unlike those seen along the higher *quais* or in the streets above.   Lone fishermen, by the score, each one apparently alone in spirit, absorbed in watching the lone line that rarely brings him up a fish, stand like monuments of patience at intervals of ten or twenty yards, unmindful of the passing boats, intent upon their tiresome, time-killing tasks of waiting for a bite.   Watching them, we recall the calmly enthusiastic declaration of the Yankee who loved fishing — "You fellers what don't fish, jest don't know what fun it is to sit, an' sit, an' sit — an' *jest fish.*"   Less numerous than the silent anglers, but just as characteristic of the city Seine, are the *tondeurs de chiens* — the men who clip, with clippers, or trim with scissors, the short hair of real dogs, or the fancy manes of those vain-looking poodles. Then too, there are the men who for a trifling fee will wash your pet dog in the Seine.   And then there are the sinister *Apaches*, who, if it suits their scheme, will send their victims "to the wash" in the murky waters of that river that swirls below the Morgue. The Apache of Paris is no Indian: he has assumed the name and acquired the blood-thirsty instincts, but he lacks the nobler attributes of the red man of the plains.   How did the "bad man," the tough, the thug of Paris get his trans-Atlantic title? He took it, so they say, from the American dime novel.   The famous thrillers, the "Nick Carter Tales" of blood and thunder

HENRI IV

which have been the inspiration of the American messenger boy, were translated into French, and republished in Paris. The gaudy pictures on the covers of those books appealed to the adventurous Bowery class of Paris. The stories suited the "bad man" of the outer boulevards, the Apache on the war-path or in quest of blood became their most honored type of lawlessness, and Nick Carter a much feared and highly respected personification of law and order. So Apache — pronounced "Apash" — in time became a synonym for the night-prowling criminal of Paris — the man who stabs and kills for the pleasure of the thing — the man who lets a woman work for him — pays her with blows, and, when in need of some excitement, waits in a dark street to strike down and rob a passer-by, more for the pleasure of the killing than for the profit of the robbing. One

THE PONT NEUF

night a gallant friend of mine, returning hotelward from a long
night of sight-seeing, was stopped in a dark street by three Apaches.
He was alone — they were in force, and therefore bold.   They
swaggered up in front of him, instead of sneaking on him from
behind.   One said, " *Tiens*, my friend, *nous sommes des Apaches—*

THE PALACE OF JUSTICE

we are Apaches!" striving to strike terror to his heart at mention
of the fearsome name.   " *Bien,* my friends," said *mon ami,* " '*c'est
bien, moi, je suis Nick Cartaire* — I am Nick Carter!" whereupon
the dumbfounded French "Indians" fled to their wigwams in
dismay.

A lecture wonderfully rich in interest could be made without
touching any part of Paris save the Isle de la Cité, which was the
cradle of Paris.   It was the site of the first cluster of Gallic huts
when France was one of the three parts of all Gaul; later it became
the fortified Roman camp when Paris bore her Latin title, Lutetia.
For centuries thereafter Paris remained a tiny town confined al-

most exclusively to this small island in the Seine; and this island is still, in truth, the "Island of the City" — is still the heart and center and therefore the most interesting part of the great Paris of to-day. It was originally cne of a group of six islands, three large and three small ones. The latter have been incorporated with it; of the former, one remains an island, the Isle St. Louis, lying a little to the east and joined to the Isle de la Cité by the Pont St. Louis; but the third and easternmost of the larger islands has become a part of the right bank, its river front now known as the Quai Henri IV. Thus the old archipelago of six low, tree-bordered isles and islets of the primitive days is now represented by two high islands, solidly walled up with masonry, loaded with buildings — among them some of the most famous piles of Paris —

A PICTURE OF THE MEDIEVAL CITÉ IN THE PALACE OF JUSTICE

and these two islands lie there in midstream like ships of stone charged deep and high with historic treasure, moored to the banks by many broad, strong chains which take the form of bridges.

Largest, if not most conspicuous, among the structures of the Cité is the Palais de Justice, nearly as wide as the island itself, stretching from quay to quay and covering nearly one-fifth of its area. On the same site there stood the stronghold of the Roman governors; there rose in a later age the Château of the Frankish kings; and there, still later, grew and flowered in all its grace and beauty the splendid Gothic palace of the crusading King, St. Louis, who died near Tunis in Africa in the year 1270. Of

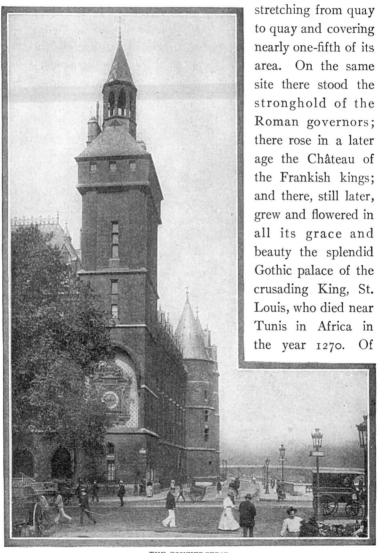

THE CONCIERGERIE

his palace there remain to-day a few notable reminders. The four towers that frown down upon the broader north branch of the Seine date from the days of Louis IX. The westernmost is called by his own name; the next is the Silver Tower; the third is Cæsar's Tower, in allusion to the days when Roman Emperors were wont to serve apprentice-ship in the art of ruling, here in this old Gallic frontier town; and the last tower, forming the northeast angle of the palace, is the famous Tour de l' Horloge, adorned with the most beautiful and elaborate old clock in Paris. The bell of that same tower sounded the signal on the night of St. Bartholomew in 1572 for the massacre of the Huguenots of the island and of the left bank, just as the bell of St. Germain l'Auxerrois had already made known

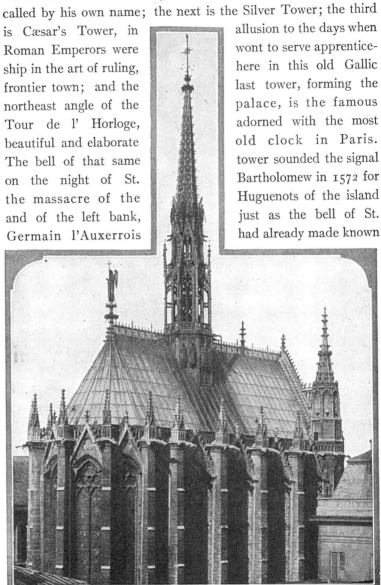

THE SAINTE CHAPELLE

to the murderers on the right bank that the king, Charles IX, had at last consented to the holy massacre planned by his grim good mother, Catherine de' Medici.

The greater part of the vast mass of buildings now known as the Palace of Justice is modern, but in exploring it the traveler,

passing from room to room, passes also from century to century. He enters the dark, low prison-cell of Marie Antoinette in the Conciergerie; he beholds court-rooms of magnificent stateliness, where sit the highest courts of the Republic; he paces the great vaulted hall known as the Salle des Pas-Perdus, where lawyers

THE WONDERFUL WINDOWS OF THE "HOLY CHAPEL"

waste or lose so many steps while pacing up and down, and waiting for a call to serve a client in the adjacent halls of justice.   But it is not until the traveler enters the Sainte Chapelle that he realizes what the beauty of the old Gothic palace must have been.   Even granting that the world-famous Holy Chapel was the most exquisite feature of the royal abode of the sainted Louis IX, the other features of the palace, harmonizing with it, as they did, must have been exquisite in grace and loveliness and impressive in dignity

THE NAVE OF NOTRE DAME

and grandeur. It is one of the architectural gems of Paris, exter-
nally as graceful and as delicate as a chiseled jewel-casket, in-
ternally as graceful and as glorious in color as if it had been made
of nothing more material than the substance of a rainbow. The
windows are wonderful — forming a Bible in stained glass —
telling in luminous color-pictures the stories of the Sacred Scrip-
tures. The Sacred Relics to enshrine which this masterpiece of
architecture was designed were nothing less precious than a fragment of the True Cross and the Crown of Thorns, which had been
worn by the Founder of Christianity on the day of the Crucifixion.
These relics, the authenticity of which was vouched for by high
ecclesiastical authority, are no longer here: they are preserved
to-day, with many other relics, in the treasury of Notre Dame.

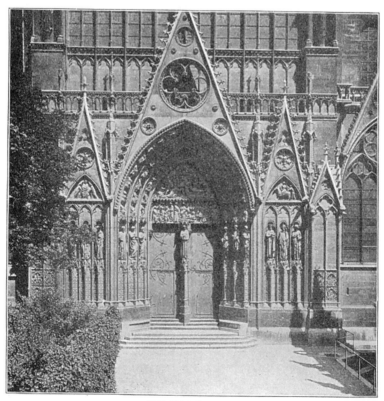

THE GOTHIC PORTAL

From the Sainte Chapelle we go to Notre Dame, the grand old church whose history is the history of Paris for the past eight hundred years. The greater part of the open space before the church — called La Place du Parvis Notre Dame — was covered

"OUR LADY OF PARIS"

formerly by hundreds of little houses and dozens of narrow medieval streets. The houses of old Paris pressed close around the most famous of her churches; but that old Paris has now disappeared, leaving the noble face of Notre Dame to look down on this empty square, from which we look up at the noble face of Notre Dame. The towers have no spires; but we do not miss them. To complete the old design by adding spires, would be to spoil this wonderful façade and rob it of that square, solid dignity that has impressed so many generations of our fellowmen. But Notre Dame is not entirely bereft of spires; a marvelously graceful one rises above the nave. It was designed by the great modern architect, Violet-le-Duc, to whose genius France owes the artistic restoration of so many of her medieval monuments. To the labors of Violet-le-Duc the world owes much. He has saved for us and for posterity many a splendid structure which, if left uncared for, would have perished, or if restored by less skilful or reverent hands would have been spoiled forever by injudicious restoration. Thanks to him, Notre Dame reveals to us to-day all the pure Gothic beauty with which she was originally endowed by the unknown architects of an artistic past — for, strange to say, of all the builders

THE CHIMERA GUARDIANS

who in successive centuries gave their best to Notre Dame, we know the name of only one — Jean de Chelles — and he was only a master-mason engaged on the work for a time in 1257.

The history of this church and its site is the history of Paris. Here stood to Jupiter in days when

an altar the old pagan Paris was a Roman strong-hold. Here also rose a lit-tle Christian church in the fourth century; in the great church that we see to-day many a King of France was crowned. Here Bonaparte crowned himself Em-peror of the French and placed a crown upon the head of Josephine. Here Napoleon III was married to the beautiful Eugénie. Here the ruffians of the Commune tried to duplicate their destructive successes at the Tuileries and the Hôtel de Ville; for having de-stroyed the palace that was

ON THE TOWERS OF NOTRE DAME

the symbol of imperial authority, and the City Hall which was the symbol of law and order, they attempted to put an end to Notre Dame, the symbol of religion. But Notre Dame was not of perishable stuff. The grand old monument refused to burn. Despite the bonfire, made of her thousands of wooden chairs and benches heaped up in the nave, the church suffered no serious

L'ECOLE DES BEAUX-ARTS

injury. To make a bonfire here was like burning a few chips in a stone fireplace. There was much smoke, some fire, a few heaps of ashes — but the old stone fireplace was scarcely warmed by the blaze. The church that had combated the eternal fires for so many centuries was not to fall a prey to those short-lived anarchistic flames.

No one should fail to climb the towers of Notre Dame. The views of Paris are superb — the stone chimeras that haunt the tower-tops are as interesting and amusing as they are horrid and uncanny. Their grimaces recall the expressions we may see on the faces of the dead folk lying in the Morgue, that sinister little building just behind Notre Dame. The derivation of the name is curious. It comes from an old French verb, "morguer," meaning "to look at solemnly," or "to look at sourly." In the old Paris prisons there was always a room called the Morgue where new prisoners were made to sit motionless for several hours in order that the police and warders might study their faces at leisure, so that they might recognize an old offender or take note of a new visage. And while subjected to this scrutiny, no doubt the prisoners wore faces as solemn and as sour as those of the victims in a modern morgue, who, all unconscious of the public stares, wait there for recognition, motionless and staring grimly at the staring crowd.

By crossing any one of the five short bridges that span the quiet, almost unused channel of the Seine that lies — rather than

MUSÉE DE CLUNY

flows, for it is locked in like a canal between the island and the left bank, *la Rive Gauche* — we may find ourselves within the vaguely defined limits of the famous Latin Quarter. It is called the Latin Quarter because it was and is the students' quarter, the part of Paris frequented by those who are following the courses in the great educational institutions, the Sorbonne, the College of France, the School of Mines, and the schools of art and architecture known collectively as *l'Ecole des Beaux-Arts*. All of these institutions are found on the south or left bank of the river, and as in the old days Latin was the language of literature and the arts, this quarter, devoted to classical studies, was called the *Quartier Latin*, or the Latin Quarter. The schools of to-day are vastly different from the original establishments to which they owe their names. The huge educational palace called La Sor-

BUILDINGS OF THE SORBONNE

bonne would never be recognized by its founder the monk, Robert of Sorbon. He was the confessor of St. Louis the King, and he began his teaching here in the year 1253, instructing sixteen young students of theology. In time, and under royal and clerical favor, his school became the supreme authority in all things touching education, sacred or pro- fane. It is to-day the seat of the University of Paris, frequented by twelve thousand students, and it is of course now free

THE TOMB OF RICHELIEU

from all religious bias, a vast temple of knowledge, no longer a stronghold of medieval dogma. In the old domed church of the Sorbonne sleeps one of the great men of France, Richelieu, cardinal and more than king, who died in 1642.

Not far from the University stands the Bibliothèque Ste. Geneviève, a modern building which suggested the design of the Public Library of Boston, but the latter is so much more effective and pleasing to the eye that its indebtedness to this Library of Ste. Geneviève is not at first apparent. Fronting on the same square is the old church of St. Etienne-du-Mont, a Gothic church, curiously overlaid with Renaissance and classical details. It looks like several different churches, inter-penetrating one another; a photograph of the façade is like a composite picture made up with pictures of many churches, each church dating from a different period. Note the curious round turret creeping up the tower, the classic pediment beneath the Gothic rose window, the thousand and one architectural contrasts and contradictions that make the exterior of St. Etienne one of the architectural marvels of old Paris. The interior is equally interesting and even more curiously beautiful. The church is now the shrine of Ste. Geneviève, who has been the sainted patroness of Paris ever since the reign of King Clovis and Queen Clotilde, whom she converted

ST. ETIENNE-DU-MONT

to Christianity about the year five hundred. She lived a life of miracles; her prayers turned back the barbarian hosts of Attila from Paris; the bed in which she slept in a cell near the Seine is said to have been left untouched by the inundation that flooded the entire quarter; — the waters formed a protecting arch over the bed of Ste. Geneviève and left it dry and undisturbed while all the rest of the neighborhood was ruined by the mire of the overflow. She died at the advanced age of eighty-nine. Her tomb is still one of the most popular objects of devotion for those who reverence the saints of old. But the gilded Gothic shrine that we see in one of the chapels of St. Etienne's church is not the one in which her bones were originally deposited, for that was of pure gold and was sent to the mint to be melted down during the Revolution. Nor does the newer shrine contain her relics, for the bones of the best-loved saint of Paris — venerated for thirteen centuries — were burned by an impious mob only about one hundred years ago. Her first tomb was in a church that stood where now the mighty Panthéon of Paris lifts its majestic dome. The Panthéon was to have been the mausoleum and monument of Ste. Geneviève, but with the passing of the Catholic Kings it became, first a Temple of Reason, then a Hall of Fame, dedicated

APPROACH TO THE TOMB OF STE. GENEVIEVE

to the great men of the fatherland, then again a church, and now, since 1885, it has become again a kind of secular Westminster Abbey, in which the great men of the nation are interred. Great thinkers sleep now in the crypt; among them Rousseau, Voltaire, and Victor Hugo, three great men whom the world has branded pagan, but whose influence has been nevertheless incalculable. Whatever may have been their faults their cry was always for "more light"; and where would progress be to-day, had it not been for the great thinkers who dared to question the great mysteries and dared to voice their questionings and to speak their thoughts?

Appropriately has Paris placed here, on a pedestal before this Temple of Free Thought, the masterpiece of the great sculptor Rodin which he calls *"Le Penseur,"* "The Thinker." The bronze colossus, type of primeval man, sits with his head bowed

THE LIBRARY OF STE. GENEVIÈVE

on his hand as if for the first time in thought. We seem to see Man, as the human animal, for the first time overwhelmed by an idea — for the first time, thought-matter has entered into and animated the coarser stuff of which the human animal is made, and Man, endowed with power to think, thinks and becomes

THE PANTHEON

conscious that he and all things sensate or insensate are but differing manifestations of that still finer matter, which we call the divine. Science is telling us to-day that all matter is divisible into still finer matter. Science has smashed the atom, once the unit of the universe, into a million atoms; each of these atoms into a million smaller atoms, for which no name has yet been found, and every one of those nameless nothings is known to be divisible into still smaller units that are not units, but merely agglomerations of matter so fine as to be inconceivable by our crude human brain. It was my privilege to meet in a famous laboratory of the Latin Quarter the one human being who from a purely scientific point of view has gone deepest into the great mystery of being. She is Mme. Curie, widow of Professor Curie and co-worker — and co-thinker — with him in the experiments that led to the discovery of radium. She now holds her late husband's chair of chemistry, and with a number of devoted

" TO THE GREAT MEN OF THE FATHERLAND "

RODIN'S " THINKER "

pupils she has probed so deeply into the mystery of the quality of matter that she has nearly reached, by purely scientific and chemical paths, the same conclusions reached by students who have approached the same mystery from the philosophical and mystical side, as for example Swedenborg, Mrs. Besant, and all who claim to have looked beyond the veil. In other words, Mme. Curie's experiments would seem to prove that what we call the spiritual world is not supernatural, but a simple, natural world of natural matter so fine as not to be perceptible to us because of the dullness of our senses and the crudeness of our organs of perception. The much-laughed-at "astral plane" of Mme. Blavatsky threatens to become the sane, matter-of-fact, and scientific-

STE. GENEVIÈVE

ally demonstrable discovery of Mme. Curie. But as we cannot yet photograph astral bodies or the scenery of the astral plane we turn our lenses now toward the very natural, quiet beings who take their thoughtful or their thoughtless ease day after day in the superb Garden of the Luxembourg — one of the many charming settings that Paris provides for those who have time to play the part of a *flâneur*. Thoroughly to enjoy the real Paris, the stranger, too, should learn the Parisian art of *flânerie*. *Flâner* is the verb that stands for "loaf," but it is a more graceful word than "loaf," and the art itself, or rather the passive state of being a *flâneur*, is far removed from the vulgarity of loafing as practiced in other less artistic countries. The art of *flânerie* is a fine art with the French, and in the parks of Paris we may observe the real Parisians, enjoying life in their own sensible and quiet way, Parisians utterly unlike those of the garish boulevards. We hear so much about the "Gay Paree" that I am tempted some day to prepare a travelogue and call it "Quiet Paris." It would make a very charming lecture. Nobody would come to hear it—but I should feel that I had paid a little of the debt I owe to Paris, by attempting to correct that almost universal misapprehension that Paris is all vanity and rush and restlessness, that the characteristic expression of Paris is a lustful leer and the chief amusement of

PALACE OF THE LUXEMBOURG

Parisians, debauchery. So it may seem, especially to the American who pays his annual toll to the vice of Paris and who has done much to perpetuate the orgy-like gayeties that animate certain sections of the city; but there is a "Quiet Paris" full of serenity and calm. This peaceful Paris is not a special quarter; it is made up of many and various fragments scattered far and wide.

The most artistic architectural fragment of that peaceful Paris of the thoughtful *flâneur* is the exquisite old palace of the Abbots of Cluny — now a museum of medieval arts and craftsmanship. The Musée de Cluny is one of the most satisfying bits of old Paris

that has survived the campaign of "improvement" that has
swept away so much of the quaintness and beauty of the past.
It is satisfying within and without.   The exterior is as charming to-day in its Gothic grace and dignity as it was when the
conscientious workmen of the abbot-builder, Jacques d'Amboise,
finished their tasks in the year 1490, and the holy men of the
Abbey of Cluny took possession of their artistic residence.   Three
centuries later the Revolution gave it to the State.   In 1833 it
became the property of the famous archeologist de Sommerard,
and when he died in 1842 the State regained possession through
purchase, and this historic house and the artistic treasures it contains may be regarded now as precious public property.   The
collections illustrate the life and customs of the Paris of the
Middle Ages and of the Renaissance, but the historic souvenirs
of the site take us back to Roman times.   Here stood the Palace
of the Cæsars when Gaul was but a Roman province.   Here
Julian was proclaimed Emperor by the soldiers of his legions

AVENUE OF THE OBSERVATORY

in the year 360, whereupon he proceeded to earn his title of
"The Apostate" by renouncing Christianity and declaring himself a champion of the old pagan gods of his ancestors. Ad-
joining the Musée de Cluny — which is a delightful, compre-
hensible epitome of the very Christian Paris
of the long Catholic centuries —
stand the ruins of the baths
of the Roman palace
which must have been,
like most things Ro-

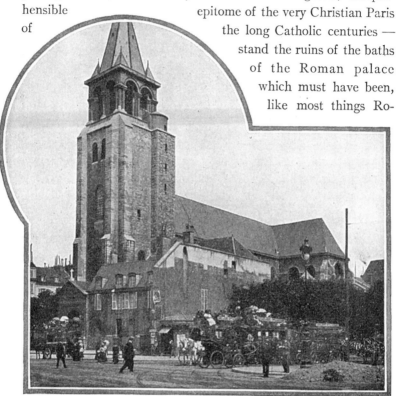

ST. GERMAIN-DES-PRÉS

man, a colossal and imposing symbol of that force that ruled
the world during the distant centuries when "Roman" was a
synonym both for "power" and for "pagan." The garden of
the museum forms a calm verdurous retreat where we may sit
and muse upon the Past — and at the same time listen to the
roar of the Present — the clamor of the Boulevard St. Germain.

Everywhere in Paris we may find calm canals of quietude
paralleling the roaring rivers of the well-known streets; or little

eddies of calm into which we may drift, out of the maelstrom of the busy boulevards — as for example the stately Avenue de l'Obsérvatoire so near the boisterous *Boul' Mich'* — the Broadway of the Latin Quarter — or the little garden under the shadow of the old church of St. Germain-des-Prés, just off the Boulevard St. Germain. You may 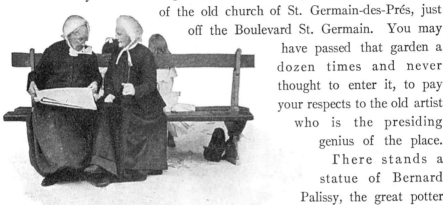 have passed that garden a dozen times and never thought to enter it, to pay your respects to the old artist who is the presiding genius of the place. There stands a statue of Bernard Palissy, the great potter and enameler, the man whose experiments, discoveries, and successes formed the foundation

THESE ALSO ARE PARISIENNES

upon which France has erected her great Ceramic Art Industry at Sèvres. Palissy was a Protestant; he died in the Bastille; but to-day his statue stands in this little garden under the shadow of the old Catholic church of St. Germain-des-Prés, which is all that is left of the ancient Abbey of St. Germain founded in 543 A. D., and at one time a veritable fortified *enceinte* where Cardinals and even Kings held sway as Abbots, in the days when the Church was in all things supreme. The battered old pile that we see to-day is a favorite subject for the painters who live in the quarter round about. There are studios in nearly every street. Behind the church we find a typical corner of Latin-Quarter Paris. The houses look as if they had "just growed" like Topsy; "just growed" as room was added to room, floor to floor, while chimneys have sprouted from each unfinished patch of wall.

Very comfortless are these old houses: comfortless in fact are

nearly all Parisian apartments when judged by the standard set
by even the more inexpensive New York flats.   Save in the new,
so-called "American quarter" on the right bank, where modern
methods of construction, heating, lighting, and "lifting" have been
introduced, Paris is hopelessly behind the age in all the big and

PALISSY, THE POTTER

little conveniences
that are looked for,
taken as a matter
of course, even in
the cheaper apart-
ment houses in our
country. Elevators
are the exception
rather than the
rule, candles are
more in evidence
than incandescent
lamps, hot water
rarely runs from
the faucets and
such a thing as
a well-equipped
bathroom is prac-
tically non-existent
in many a building
occupied by people of the better class.   Never shall I forget the
trouble and excitement occasioned by my attempt, some years
ago, to get a real hot bath in the lodgings I had taken — before
discovering that there was no modern plumbing on the premises.
"Un bain, Monsieur?   Mais parfaitement!   I will make the bath
to come at five o'clock this afternoon," said the obliging *concierge*
when I expressed a desire for total immersion.   "But I want the
bath now, this morning, before breakfast," I insisted.   "Impos-
sible, Monsieur, it requires time to prepare and to bring, but

it will be superb — your bath — the last gentleman who took
one a month ago enjoyed his very much. You will see, Monsieur, that when one orders a bath in Paris, one gets a beautiful
bath — it will be here at four o'clock." At four, a man, or
rather a pair of legs, came staggering up my stairs — five
flights, by the way — with a full-sized zinc bath tub, inverted
and concealing the head and shoulders and half the body of
the miserable owner of those legs. The tub was planted in
the middle of my room: a white linen lining was adjusted;
sundry towels and a big bathing sheet, to wrap myself in
after the ordeal, were ostentatiously produced. Then came the
all-important operation of filling the tub. Two pails, three

WHERE ARTISTS DWELL

servants, and countless trips down to the hydrant, several floors below, at last did the trick: the tub was full of ice-cold water. "But I ordered a hot bath." "Patience, Monsieur, behold here is the hot water!" Whereupon the bath man opens a tall zinc cylinder that looks like a fire extinguisher and pours about two gallons of hot water into that white-lined tub — result a tepid bath — expense sixty cents — time expended two hours, for the tub had to be emptied by dipping out the

HOW YOUR BATH TUB COMES —

A "LEFT BANK" STREET

— AND GOES

water and carrying it away, pail after pail. Then the proud owner of the outfit slung his pails on his arms, put his tub on his head like a hat, and began the per-

IN AN ETCHER'S STUDIO

ilous descent of my five flights of stairs. I had had enough
of primitive Paris — I moved to costlier quarters where tubbing
was not wonderingly regarded as an Anglo-Saxon extravagance,
to be indulged in more as a matter of monthly ostentation than
as a joyful daily duty.

As for the telephone system of Paris it is an irritating joke.
Why try to telephone when time is precious and taxicabs cheap?
The telegraph system, under Government ownership and manage-
ment, is absurdly inadequate, and so untrustworthy are the em-
ployees that if you really want your messages transmitted you ask
for, receive, and *pay for* a receipt which insures you against the
probability of having your money pocketed and your wire sent
via the waste basket. The *reçu* costs two cents but spares you
many an hour of uncertainty. Some things they do not " man-
age better in France," the telephone and telegraph being among
them. It is said that we love men for their faults; and we may say
the same of nations or of cities; most of the failings of France

and Paris are delightful failings—picturesque or temperamental faults that inspire admiration or affection. We would not have our Paris other than it is. Happily, it is not yet a modern city; the Latin Quarter is still in many ways delightfully medieval, and that is why we love it and why it is the favorite haunt of

A STUDY IN GABLES

artists. They can find in Paris "inspiration," "atmosphere," "temperament,"— all those things that artists talk so much about, but never can define; and they can find here in the same city a market for their wares, buyers for their goods — rich patrons of the arts; for just across the river lies the " Gay Paree" which is peopled every season by the Crœsuses of the New World who come to spend the crude gold of the New World, not only in buying Parisian pleasures, but also in purchasing pictures painted in studios perched high among the housetops of this older Paris. Crœsus, by the way, is the only million-aire of his period whose name has come down to us: and why is Crœsus remembered? Not because he was rich, but be-cause he was a patron of the arts. Although we have not the

IN A STUDIO

wealth of Crœsus, we like to pose as patrons of our artist friends in Paris. It is always pleasant to drop into, or rather climb up to, the studio of some good friend and criticize his latest picture, look over his new etchings, and hear him tell modestly about the things that he has done and the things that he in-tends to do; and every year we find him doing better, bigger things, and one year we find that the enthusiastic boy we knew as a struggling toiler in the long school of art has become somebody — has made a name — that the Salon accepts his pictures, that his pictures all find purchasers; and we begin to realize that the etching of an old street in an old *quartier* that he sent as a gift a few years ago now has a value — aside from that value that everything well done possesses — not merely because it was a gift, but because other prints from the same plate have since

From an Etching by Herman A. Webster.

"LA RUE BRISE MICHE"

won both praise and prizes in great exhibitions or a place in the collections of great connoisseurs. It represents a narrow street in the old quarter of Paris, known as *Le Marais*. You will say at first that no such quaint old street exists to-day in Paris; but the artist himself will take you to it; you may take your camera, and the camera will take a

THE ETCHER'S WINDOW

LA RUE BRISE MICHE AS REVEALED BY THE CAMERA

picture of that quaint old street, *La Rue Brise Miche,* showing it as it appears to-day, and every day, to any one who takes the trouble to find it — by first losing himself in the labyrinth of the old Quarter of the Marsh. You cannot know your Paris until you have been guided through the *Quartier du Marais* and other queer old quarters by some painter or some etcher who has explored them in his search for subjects such as this. These quarters are still quaint even in photographs.

This suggests that there is still another Paris to be done into a travelogue some day — "Old Paris" or "Quaint Paris," the Paris of the artist, or preferably of the art student — for that Paris still has some right to its old title, *La Bohème.* But Parisian "Bohemia" is not a place, a quarter, or a district of the city — the real Parisian Bohemia may be defined as "a personal pecuniary condition." Bohemia is where men get their money's worth. Bohemians are those who refuse to pay more in money or in time — and time is money — to pay more for anything than it is worth. Bohemianism, the right sort, means simply

AT THIRION'S — UPSTAIRS

"MARIUS"

common sense; a sensible Bohemian saying is "Why pay ten francs for a dinner on the right bank when one can dine so well for twenty *sous* at Thirion's on the left? Thirion's is in the Boulevard St. Germain; it is frequented by the students, poets, and painters of the *quartier* and from time to time by tourist parties from the fashionable hotels, guided usually by some ex-art-student of the years that are no more. The place has been historic ever since some one invented the story that Thackeray used to come here when he lived in Paris, and that the walls are covered with the scribblings and the autographs of Thackeray and the famous personages of his time. The walls are now discreetly covered with burlap; the precious writing on the wall is never shown. Instead, paintings by impecunious patrons are displayed for sale. When one is sold, there is much rejoicing, and a new meal-ticket is issued to the happy painter, while Marius — dear old Marius, once merely the waiter, now the son-in-law and successor of the late-lamented Thirion — goes to the tube and shouts an order to the kitchen. The words that travel oftenest down the tube are these, "*Un soixante-quinze, saignant, pommes pailles.*" Literally, "One seventy-fiver — bleeding — straw potatoes." Real meaning of the phrase — a little beefsteak that costs seventy-five centimes — fifteen cents — smothered in Julienne potatoes, called *pommes pailles*, because a heap of them looks like a pile of straw. How many glad,

AT THIRION'S — DOWNSTAIRS

young, empty, and ar-
tistic stomachs have
rejoiced to hear good
Marius sing down this
tube with phonographic
accent, born of a mil-
lion repetitions, *"Un
soixante-quinze, saig-
nant, pommes pailles!"*

Downstairs on the
ground floor a bust of
old man Thirion, done
by a sculptor-patron,
possibly in payment for
many meals, looks down
on tables usually occu-

"IT IS THE HEALTH"

pied by rank outsiders, for those who know the place go up that
spiral stairway in the corner to the *entresol* where the artistic
atmosphere is thicker. Not much more pretentious
in aspect, but far more famous among epicures who
are not compelled to count the cost of the good
cheer of Paris, is another restaurant, known as
La Tour d'Argent and renowned for its cuisine.
All things they do well at the Tower of Silver —
but few patrons care to order aught but the
"dîner de la maison" — with its three marvelous
courses — *Potage Tour d'Argent, — Sole Car-
dinale, — Canneton à la Presse* — the last being
the dish upon which the house rests its fame
and stakes its reputation. It is prepared and
served with an almost religious solemnity by the
distinguished-looking proprietor of the establishment, Frédéric Delair — "Frédéric the Great of
Paris" he is called by those who have partaken

SOFT DRINKS

of the famous duck done as Frédéric alone can do it. Patrons
who come for the first time never fail to remark the fact that
Frédéric looks like the late Dr. Ibsen. He dissects ducks as
skilfully as the great Norwegian dramatist dissected human
character. Every duck he serves is numbered; every party
receives a   certificate giving the   number

FRÉDÉRIC THE GREAT, OF THE TOUR
D'ARGENT

of the   bird;
ours was   No. 28,556,
and it was just   as good as the
twenty-eight   thousand five
hundred and fifty-five *cannetons* that had previously passed
through the *presse* operated so skilfully by the famous old man of
the famous *Restaurant de la Tour d'Argent*.

Parisian cooking is both a fine art and a science, and no
traveler who appreciates this fact can pass the building of the
Institute of France without vaguely wondering why that famous
institution has not among its many illustrious divisions an *Académie Nationale de la Cuisine*.

The Institute comprises five academies — *Inscriptions et*

Belles-lettres, Sciences, Beaux-arts, Sciences morales et politiques,
and possibly most important, surely most celebrated, the French
Academy, *l'Académie Française*, with its membership of forty
living Immortals — and its necrologic lists of names that have
adorned French literature during the last three centuries. The
Académie Française was founded by Cardinal Richelieu in
1635 for the perfecting of the French language and the advance-
ment of literature. Its members are called "Immortals" because
each is supposed to have accomplished something that will give
him everlasting fame. Yet the names of many members are
practically unknown outside of France, while men whose fame is
world-wide have been refused admission. We look in vain for
the name of Molière among the Immortals of his generation, and
in our own day Emile Zola, with superb audacity, time and again

THE INSTITUTE

THE BOOK STALLS OF THE " BOUQUINISTES "

announced himself a candidate for the place left vacant each time an Immortal put on immortality, but as often as Zola proclaimed his right to a seat among the famous forty, the Académie proceeded to elect some man less famous, leaving the great hero of the Dreyfus case out in the cold — too great, too big, too popular, and too famous to be admitted to the Institute he had learned to scorn, but at the door of which he never ceased to knock, for his reputation's sake — and

LITERATURE ALONG THE SEINE

also, we suspect, for the fun of the thing. Literature is very much
in evidence along the quays on the left bank of the Seine. On
every parapet rest the boxes of the *bouquinistes*, the men or
women who deal in books both old and new, but always second-
hand. Their stalls form a continuous book-shop about two miles
long — a shop of many score of proprietors — of many thousand

ST. GERMAIN L'AUXERROIS, FROM THE LOUVRE

volumes, of very modest value. Two or three cents will buy a
decent work by a famous writer — even the less decent works of
more famous writers sell for modest sums, but the most numerous
frequenters of the *bouquinistes* are those who merely pause to
browse on books — free-gratis-for-nothing — as, on their way to
or from their daily tasks they loiter up or down the open-air
corridors of this "Public Library of the Passer-by."

A famous foot-bridge — called the *Pont des Arts* — leads
from the Institute, which is the home of the Science and the
Letters of France, to the Louvre, which is the home of much that

is best of the Art of the entire world. It contains the largest,
richest, and most fascinating art collection ever gathered together
under one roof in any city of the ancient or the modern world.
I say, under one roof, but the Louvre has many roofs. The
Louvre is not a palace — it is a palatial city, a suite of variously
beautiful constructions dating from different periods, differing
one from another in architectural design. The finest feature is
the east façade with its twenty-eight Corinthian columns, built
during the reign of Louis XIV, about two hundred and fifty years
ago. This is, however, comparatively new. The oldest building
that bore the name of Louvre dates back eight hundred years.
It was a hunting lodge of the French Kings; this part of Paris
was then a forest, and here they hunted wolves, or *loups*, hence,
so say some authorities, the name "Louvre"—a strange name

THE EAST FAÇADE OF THE LOUVRE

THE VENUS OF MELOS

for the richest art museum in the world. To try to put the collection of the Louvre into a travelogue would be hopelessly absurd; but we cannot turn away without rendering homage to that marble Queen and Empress who from her pedestal in this palace of so many vanished Queens and Empresses reigns over the whole world of beauty. She stands at the end of a long marble corridor. To come into the lovely presence of that goddess from the island of Melos we pass between two ranks of lesser goddesses, modestly yielding to her the throne of supreme beauty to which any one of them might aspire, were it not for her.

It is difficult for the traveler to tell just where the Louvre ends and where the Palace of the Tuileries begins — for these two historic homes of French royalty now form one vast connected series of palaces and pavilions. The two long wings of the combined palaces inclose three great open spaces that are divided from one another only in name — the inner Garden of the Louvre, adorned with modern sculpture — the great paved area

PLACE DU CARROUSEL AND THE LOUVRE

called the Place du Carrousel, dominated by the smaller Napoleonic arch of triumph, and the broad, beautiful expanse that forms the beginning of the broader and longer Garden of the Tuileries that stretches all the way to the Place de la Concorde. Formerly the old original Palace of the Tuileries, begun by Catherine de' Medeci in 1564, closed the now open space between the two pavilions that now terminate the wings of the Tuileries on the west. It was the home of royal and imperial glories and tragedies. Before the Revolution it was not the chief royal residence, but in 1789 Louis XVI was brought hither from Versailles and installed as a hostage of the nation. Three years later,

thirty thousand armed men broke into the Tuileries and forced
the King to put the red cap of the Revolution on his head; then,
on the decisive tenth of August, 1792, Louis and Marie Antoinette
fled from another mob, leaving their Swiss Guard of about eight
hundred men to be massacred by the angry populace.   After the
awful Reign of Terror came the glo-
rious Empire of Napoleon
the Great, with the Tui-
leries as its imperial
court. After Water-
loo came the Res-
toration with
Louis XVIII in
the Tuileries as
Bourbon King.
His successor,
Charles X, was
driven from the
palace by the rev-
olutionists of 1830.
His successor, Louis
Philippe, was forced to
fly thence during the revolution in 1848. Napoleon

THE FRIEND OF THE BIRDS

III revived the glories of the Tuileries, and here his consort
Eugénie reigned as Empress of the French until he met his great
defeat at Sedan in the Franco-Prussian War, when, aided by her
American friend, Dr. Evans, she in turn fled from the palace
which had seen so many sovereigns put to flight by the fickle
populace of Paris.   And finally, at the end of the anarchic period
that followed the withdrawal of the German troops from Paris,
the mobs of the Commune, on the point of defeat, wreaking their
vengeance on all the public buildings of the Capital, filled the
Tuileries with combustibles and applied the torch.   When the

Government troops, coming from Versailles, forced their way into the city, this home of Kings and Emperors had become a scorched and shattered wreck, a splendid stone and marble wreck which has since been cleared away. It is interesting to remember that the stones of the wrecked palace were purchased by the descendants of the great Napoleon's arch enemy, Pozzo di Borgo of Corsica, and transported to Ajaccio, where one pavilion of the Tuileries has been reërected as the country house of the Pozzo di Borgo family. Thus, part of the very palace to which "the little Corsican" fought his way through seas of blood now shelters the offspring of his bitterest enemy, who from its windows look down from their Corsican hillside upon the Corsican city where Napoleon was born. See how the tangle of historic threads gets thicker and thicker with every step we take into the past of this wonderful Paris.

THE ARCH OF THE CARROUSEL

At the western end of the Jardin des Tuileries there is a charming shady terrace, from which we may look down upon the grandest public square in the world, the Place de la Concorde. That terrace is one of the most delightful bits of the "Quiet Paris," which should be sought out by every visitor who wishes

CHAMPS-ÉLYSÉES

PLACE DE

really to know and enjoy this city by the Seine as it should be known and enjoyed. So warm and sunny is this terrace, even in winter time, that Frenchmen call it lovingly *La Petite Provence* — "Little Provence"— as we might call a sunny spot in Central Park our "Little Florida."

The glorious Place de la Concorde owes its name, "The Place of the Peace," to the peace signed at Aix-la-Chapelle in 1748, during the reign of Louis XV, an equestrian statue of whom was set up here, only to be pulled down in 1792 when the great square was renamed Place de la Révolution. It was indeed *the* place of the Revolution — the place of the Reign of Terror,

the place of many executions, some of which were merely mur-
ders — the place of the Guillotine. History has done a grievous
wrong to a certain worthy Dr. Guillotin in crediting him with
the invention of the contrivance that bears his name. He was
not the inventor of the guillotine — he was the man who recom-

LA CONCORDE   JARDIN DES TUILERIES

mended its use in order to render decapitations less uncertain,
less revolting — more mercifully quick. The inventor was a
certain equally worthy Dr. Louis, and the machine he made for
cutting off heads with neatness and dispatch was called at first
the "Louisette," but when the Constituant Assembly acted upon
the recommendation of Dr. Guillotin, his name attached itself
inseparably and forever to the thing for which it stands to-day —
and became a name to shudder at. It began its work in this
square with the highest: the head of the King was the first head
severed in the Place de la Concorde; then one by one, and later,
lot by lot, fell the heads of the great and famous, cleft from bowed

shoulders by the swift-falling blade: Charlotte Corday, Marie Antoinette, Philippe Égalité, father of the future King Louis Philippe; then Danton, and finally even Robespierre placed their heads beneath the gliding blade and their troubled spirits glided out of this world's turmoil. For each the last vision of our world was this wonderful great square; but the next vision — the first vision that greeted their spirit eyes as they opened on a world that we cannot see — was it the same for each? Or did each soul find — beyond the guillotine — the kind of world which it had fashioned for itself? The exact location of that scaffold is marked by one of the two fountains, the one nearest the

THE OBELISK OF LUXOR

Seine. There stood that terrible machine from which flowed, like red wine from a winepress, the best and the worst blood of the French nation. But we are not here to conjure up these dreadful memories of a dark yesterday; we come to see and to enjoy the Paris of

ONE OF THE FOUNTAINS

to-day in all her brilliant splendor. Still there
is no escaping historical associations. We
turn from the reminders of the Revolution
and find ourselves confronted by a reminder
of the Franco-Prussian War, the statue representing the city of Strasbourg, lost to France
in 1871. It is one of the eight statues
that surround the Place de la Concorde
and represent eight of the chief provin-
cial cities; those cities are Rouen and
Brest, Bordeaux and Nantes, Marseilles
and Lyons, Lille and Strasbourg. The
Strasbourg monument is always draped
with mourning emblems and adorned

"MERCURY"

with wreaths of immortelles as if in memory of a dear sister who

CHURCH OF THE MADELEINE

is dead. Every year these dec-
orations are renewed by the
patriotic French; but meantime
Strasbourg lives and prospers
under the flag that Bismarck
raised above her. And more
historical associations greet us
as we turn toward the middle
of the square. There stands the
obelisk that sends our thoughts
far up the Nile to Luxor, — ancient Thebes, — where we saw
the twin of this Egyptian mon-
olith standing before the temple
of Great Ramses in the city that
was the Paris of the Pharaohs.

"MILITAIRES"

The Obelisk of Luxor tells us in hieroglyphics that very few can
read — and at which very few

IN THE AVENUE DES CHAMPS-ÉLYSÉES

LE GRAND PALAIS DES BEAUX–ARTS

even pause to cast a glance — of the glory

of King Ramses II, who reigned in Egypt more than three thousand years ago. Astonishing, is it not, that to-day — even to-day — the traveler may meet Ramses face to face in Cairo, where in a glass case, in the National Museum, we may gaze at the actual features of the man who caused the obelisk to be quarried and caused a record of his deeds to be cut deep

ONE OF THE ENTRANCES

LE PETIT PALAIS

in its stony surfaces. The mummied body of Ramses the Great
bids fair to last as long as his great granite monuments. We
know that he loved display; that he was a vain and ostentatious
King. He could ask no better setting for the stone that glorifies
his name; it is set in the grandest square of the world's most
monumentally decorative city, at the head of the wide Champs-
Élysées, the greatest avenue of vanity and glory in the modern

COURT OF THE "LITTLE PALACE"

world. At the far end of that avenue is the great Arch of
Napoleon: the self-designed memorial
of the ancient King of Egypt faces the
self-commanded memorial of the
modern Emperor of Europe, and
the Arch says to the Obelisk,
"Ramses, I understand *you*,"
and the Obelisk replies, "Yes,
Bonaparte — we understand
each other." From the Obelisk thirty-two centuries look
down upon the Champs-
Élysées. The street vistas
of Paris are overwhelming in
their suggestions of magnificence. There is an antique
splendor about Paris — a glory
that can never fade — that makes

THE ALEXANDER BRIDGE

her seem a sister city to the imperial cities of the past, to Thebes and Alexandria, Athens and Rome; she is in aspect the one, the only, Imperial City of the present day, and Paris grows more splendid from year to year. In preparation for the Exposition of 1900 a great transformation was wrought in the quarter

A PRIVATE "HÔTEL" IN THE CHAMPS-ÉLYSÉES

that lies between the Champs-Élysées and the Esplanade des Invalides. The old Palais de l'Industrie, which had been the home of the Salon for so many years, was demolished, and on and near the site there rose two beautiful buildings, Le Petit Palais and Le Grand Palais des Beaux-Arts. Between them is the wide Avenue Nicholas II, leading to the superb Pont Alexandre III, grandest of all the bridges that span the River Seine. Magnificent are the glimpses of Paris from this and from other bridges.

Happily for the traveler, the grandest and most splendid spectacles of Paris are all free. For nothing, we may enjoy these vistas of magnificence: and those glorious moments just at sunset, when Paris is transfigured by the magic lights and colors of the sky, are free as air to all who care to look. But even without the trickery of color, Paris is grandiose, the Arc de Triomphe is imposing even in the crude white light of noon. We look at it always with increasing admiration. It grows in majesty each time that we behold it. The finest of the four colossal groups that adorn the arch, represents the Goddess of War, Bellona, sister of the War God, Mars, leading her warriors to combat. She seems to be advancing like a whirlwind; we almost hear her cry, a cry that must be like that of the *Walküre*. The Germans, when they marched around this arch in 1871, must have looked

ÉLYSÉE-PALACE HÔTEL AND A SUBWAY ENTRANCE

up in admiration at this glorious female fiend and likened her to the mythical Valkyrs of the Fatherland. I say when the Germans marched *around* the arch, for I am told that they did not march through or under it. The German Kaiser, William the Great, who had just been crowned Emperor in the Palace at Versailles and whose troops were about to enter Paris in triumph, gave order that the line of march should lead around, not through, the arch, thus courteously sparing the French nation a cruel humiliation. It is affirmed that after the conquering hosts had passed, the French brought out deodorizing carts and secretly sprinkled with disinfectants all the streets through which the Teutonic troops had

"WAR"

THE ARCH OF TRIUMPH

marched, to wash away the stain, or, as I once jestingly ventured to say on the platform, "to kill the germs from Germany." Of course, I meant this as a joke, or rather an allusion to the well-known joke about "Parasites from Paris, Microbes from Ireland and Germs from Germany," but a fatherland-loving, un-comprehending German citizen of the city

A SIDE VIEW OF THE ARCH

where I used the phrase, would not let pass what he regarded as

AVENUE DE LA GRANDE ARMÉE

an affront to his victorious compatriots. He sought me out behind the scenes and boiling with Weber-Fieldian indignation he assured me that "Ven dey make a marsch in Paris dose German soldiers dey don't no germs on de ground leave! So dot vashing it vas necessary *not!*"

The Arch is more than a hundred and fifty feet in height and although begun during Napoleon's reign it was not finished until

THE CHAMPS-ELYSÉES FROM THE ARCH

1836 when Louis Philippe was King. Inscribed upon it are the names of one hundred and seventy-two battles — all Napoleonic victories — and the names of three hundred and eighty-six generals, all victors through the genius of Napoleon.

From the Arch, two of the twelve splendid avenues that radiate from the Place de l'Etoile lead to the Bois de Boulogne. We may follow the wide Avenue de la Grande Armée — which is really an extension of the Champs-Élysées, under a different name — to the Porte Maillot, just beyond which at certain seasons we find the crowds and tumult of the Fête de Neuilly, or we may follow the more aristocratic Avenue du Bois de Boulogne, which is the approach to the famous park most favored by the fashionable. One private palace in that avenue always arrests the attention of the American visitor. It is the Parisian domicile of Mme. la Duchesse de Talleyrand, née Anna Gould. It was erected under the artistic supervision of her first husband, M. le Comte Boni de Castellane, and is — to a more or less conspicuous degree — a reproduction of a celebrated little palace at Versailles, *le Grand Trianon*, built two centuries ago by Louis XIV for Mme. de Maintenon. Both are dainty structures of a pale pinkish tone; the modern palace a trifle nobler in design, the older palace more effective because of its broad terraces and lovely gardens, to reproduce which in Paris would have cost more than even the richest of trans-Atlantic heiresses could afford   to spend upon a home in the Old World.

AVENUE DU BOIS DE BOULOGNE

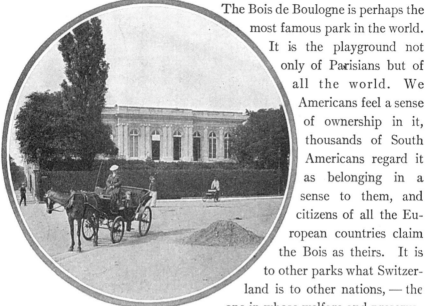

THE GOULD-DE CASTELLANE TRIANON
IN PARIS

The Bois de Boulogne is perhaps the most famous park in the world. It is the playground not only of Parisians but of all the world. We Americans feel a sense of ownership in it, thousands of South Americans regard it as belonging in a sense to them, and citizens of all the European countries claim the Bois as theirs. It is to other parks what Switzerland is to other nations, — the one in whose welfare and preservation the entire world is interested.

THE GRAND TRIANON AT VERSAILLES

In the midst of the Bois there is, or rather was, one of the most delightful little private estates in the world, the Château de Bagatelle, — built in a month by the Comte d'Artois, who later became King Charles X, in order to win a wager he had made

A PARISIAN PALACE BUILT WITH FOREIGN GOLD

with his royal sister-in-law, Marie Antoinette. Over the entrance to the little palace he set the words, "Parva sed apta," and it was undoubtedly this dainty dwelling that du Maurier had in mind when he wrote of the artistic dream-experiences of Peter Ibbetson in that most wonderful of novels — most wonderful, at least, to those who think they understand.

Until 1904, when it was purchased for six and a half million francs by the municipality of Paris from the heirs of Sir Richard Wallace, to whom the Bagatelle had belonged for many years,

and opened to the public, this fascinating *demeure* was like a
mysterious, forbidden paradise, hidden   in
the verdure of the Bois, surrounded
by high walls and known only to
those who, in the course of curious
wanderings in the wood had
come to its walls and skirted
them from one gate to another,
peering in through each in a
vain effort to gain some idea
of what the Bagatelle was like.
I have always had, like all
other men, the secret hope that
some day I might suddenly ac-
quire countless millions; whereupon my first wise extravagance
would have been to make the Baga-

THE CASCADE OF THE BOIS

telle my own, fill it again with art treasures as Sir Richard Wallace did, and dwell there in that little palace, "Parva sed apta," set in the midst of that lovely private park which was *in* but not *of* the public Bois, — so near to Paris, yet so tranquil in its beautiful

THE RESTAURANT IN THE PRÉ CATELAN

seclusion. But Paris has possessed herself of my dream château, and now, even without the millions, I am free to sit beneath the old trees or upon the stately terrace, and in the quiet hours when there are no other *flâneurs* within the gates, pretend that, after all, the Bagatelle belongs to me. 'Tis better to have dreamed and waked than never to have dreamed at all.

Within sight of my lost paradise lies the broad expanse of Longchamps — the long fields — to which all Paris, "*tout Paris*," comes in its very best clothes to see the famous race for the Grand

Prix — and incidentally to be thrilled by the beauty, variety, and daring of the costumes worn by the women. On the day of one great turf event we quite forgot to look at the horses in our

THE BAGATELLE

admiration for the pretty clothes on view, and after careful scrutiny of the assembled *toilettes* we chose as the most delightfully *chic* — the most characteristically Parisian figures in the fashionable throng—the two that appear in the picture on the next page. Imagine the amazement and the patriotic thrill with which I learned a few months later, through a friend who chanced to

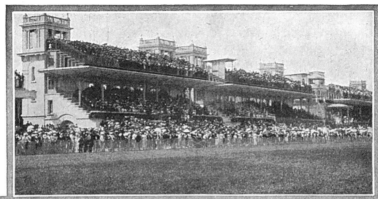

AT THE RACES

recognize the ladies in the picture, that both are Americans, and that both frocks were designed and made by a dressmaker in Fifth Avenue — and one frock is of Irish lace !

The great annual review of the garrison of

Paris is held on the field of Longchamps. A striking feature of recent reviews has been the appearance of the military airships soaring over the heads of the assembled troops. Yet the newest dirigible is not more wonderful in our eyes than were the clumsy, helpless bags of gas used by the aeronauts of 1870 during the siege of Paris. A monument has been erected near the Porte des Ternes to commemo-

WINGED MESSENGERS

rate their exploits, and to bear grateful testimony to the services rendered the besieged by the carrier-pigeons who faithfully delivered messages beyond the German lines. This monument, by Bartholdi, is remarkable in its successful suggestion of a soaring balloon, around which bronze birds seem actually to flutter, barely touching the bronze envelope with the tips of their bronze wings.

IN MEMORY OF THE
AERONAUTS AND THE
CARRIER-PIGEONS OF 1870

But of all the monuments of Paris not one so completely dominates the city as the Eiffel Tower — that inverted exclamation point — nearly a thousand feet in height. From the top Paris looks like a model city of tiny toy houses, tiny green trees marking the squares and parks and boulevards, a narrow, glittering ribbon marking the curving course of the River Seine. Here and there looms something slightly larger play-thing, — a toy arch of triumph or a toy opera-house. We feel a childish desire to reach down and pick up bits of that pretty, silent, toy-like Paris to take home with us as souvenirs, and could we do so we would reach first for that brightest, glittering thing that lies like a glorious, golden bubble near the open space which we recognize as the Esplanade des Invalides. That golden object is the world-famous dome beneath which sleeps the world-famous man who was born in Corsica, conquered Europe, died in St. Helena, and, according to his dying wish, lies buried on the banks of the Seine in the midst of the French

THE EIFFEL TOWER

people whom he had loved so well. The dome was constructed more than two hundred years ago and used as a royal chapel attached to the church of St. Louis-des-Invalides, which of course was a part of the great institution called the Hôtel des

FROM ONE OF THE ELEVATORS

Invalides — not a hospital, as the name suggests, but a home for old soldiers, founded by Louis XIV. It once sheltered seven thousand aged pensioners; now there are only eighteen "invalides" lodged there, for the greater part of the vast building is used as a military museum. The tomb itself, in the crypt under the dome, was not completed until 1853, although the remains of the great Emperor had been brought to Paris in 1840, nearly twenty years after his death in exile on that South Atlantic island where, a thousand miles from the coast of Africa, he had lived for nearly six years as the "Prisoner of St. Helena." It is now possible to contrast the simple grandeur of this tomb with the crude simplicity of the tomb in which he lay for so many years at St. Helena. The stone slabs that were taken from the

FROM THE TOP OF THE EIFFEL TOWER

kitchen fireplace of Longwood — his home of exile — to form the first tomb for the dead world-conqueror in the *Vallée du Géranium*, have been brought recently to Paris, and that simple, temporary tomb of gray, plebeian stone has been reconstructed in one of the chapels of the great church wherein the body of the Little Corporal now lies in its grandiose, everlasting, imperially purple sarcophagus. The inscription on the old tomb from St. Helena is merely a line from Lamartine,

ICI GÎT . . . POINT DU NOM

That was all, because Sir Hudson Lowe, the crabbed English jailer of the Corsican Cæsar, would not permit them to inscribe upon the tomb of his dead prisoner any imperial title — so the friends of the departed Emperor inscribed thereon that one line which means,

HERE LIES . . . NO NAME

knowing full well that the whole world would know that there lay one so great and famous that no name nor title on his tomb could add a jot to his great glory and renown.

An unearthly light falling from unseen windows high above, upon the mosaic pave-ment of the crypt, there re-veals the inlaid letters that spell the names of eight now famous places all of which, save one, would be unknown to fame had not Napoleon chosen them as battle-fields and there won amazing victories that changed the desti-nies of many nations.

With the great Napoleon asleep be-neath the Dôme des Invalides, Europe now fears France no more. Think of the energy, determin-ation, obstinacy, pride, wisdom, and tireless industry of

THE RESTING PLACE OF NAPOLEON BONAPARTE

the man imprisoned now in that sarcophagus of porphyry. In it lies the mortal body of the most masterful man the world has seen since Julius Cæsar. His story reads to-day like the fable of some mythic god—for he performed impossibilities, accomplished things that no other man would have dared attempt. Some day I hope to make a pictorial epitome of the life-story of Napoleon, and pictures to illustrate that amazing story must be brought from the ends of the Old World,—from Egypt and from Italy, from Corsica and Spain, from Austria and Germany, from Poland and the steppes of Russia, — for Napoleon touched all these lands, set his stamp upon them, and altered the currents of their history. What an enthralling task it should be to follow the world-conqueror from Corsica, through many victories, to the Tuileries—and from the throne, through many victories and a few defeats, to St. Helena — and from St. Helena back in the triumph of death to this mausoleum, in this great city of Paris that he made so glorious.

NAPOLEON I

The Paris of to-day never could have become the Paris that it is but for the great Napoleon, who poured the treasures of the world into the lap of the city he loved so well. To him Paris owes much of her modern splendor; to him France owes her age of greatest glory; to him the world itself owes a great debt of gratitude because he, more than any other man, made clear the hollow futility of Tradition. Napoleon dealt Tradition a death-blow, he broke the bonds of ancient usage, he taught men that a man is not what he is born, but what he makes himself. He was the first great *individual* of our modern age, — the age when man looks within himself for power and for guidance, the age when *individuality* is everything.

Further Reading

Several popular Paris guidebooks contain excellent historical information about the buildings, monuments, and areas of the city, including Eugene Fodor's *Exploring Paris* (1995) and Arthur Frommer's *Paris* (1996). Frommer's approach is more personal, and his volume has a wonderful comparison of the Left Bank and the Right Bank. See also Thomas Carlson-Reddig's *An Architect's Paris* (1993). Reddig's illustrations are superb, as is his bibliography.

Anyone who wishes to find out about the major events and personalities of Europe between 1875 and 1914 should read Eric Hobsbawn's *The Age of Empire: 1875-1914* (1989). Other interesting books on the period include *Europe 1815-1914* by Gordon Craig; James Joll's *Europe Since 1870;* and *A Survey of European Civilization* (Vol. II, from 1660), by Wallace K. Ferguson and Geoffrey Brown. See also: Barbara Tuchman, *The Proud Tower* (1966); Edward R. Tannenbaum, *1900: The Generation Before the Great War* (1976); and *War by Timetable: How the First World War Began* (1969), *The Struggle for Mastery in Europe, 1848-1918* (1971), and *The Last of Old Europe: A Grand Tour* (1976), by A. J. P. Taylor.

—Dr. Fred L. Israel

CONTRIBUTORS

General Editor FRED L. ISRAEL is an award-winning historian. He received the Scribe's Award from the American Bar Association for his work on the Chelsea House series *The Justices of the United States Supreme Court.* A specialist in American history, he was general editor for Chelsea's *1897 Sears Roebuck Catalog.* Dr. Israel has also worked in association with Arthur M. Schlesinger, jr. on many projects, including *The History of U.S. Presidential Elections* and *The History of U.S. Political Parties.* He is senior consulting editor on the Chelsea House series *Looking into the Past: People, Places, and Customs,* which examines past traditions, customs, and cultures of various nations.

Senior Consulting Editor ARTHUR M. SCHLESINGER, JR. is the preeminent American historian of our time. He won the Pulitzer Prize for his book *The Age of Jackson* (1945), and again for *A Thousand Days* (1965). This chronicle of the Kennedy Administration also won a National Book Award. He has written many other books, including a multi-volume series, *The Age of Roosevelt.* Professor Schlesinger is the Albert Schweitzer Professor of Humanities at the City University of New York, and has been involved in several other Chelsea House projects, including the *American Statesmen* series of biographies on the most prominent figures of early American history.

IRVING WALLACE (1916-1990), whose essay on Burton Holmes is reprinted in the forward to The World 100 Years Ago, is one of the most widely read authors in the world. His books have sold over 200 million copies, and his best-sellers include *The Chapman Report, The Prize, The Man, The Word, The Second Lady,* and *The Miracle.*

INDEX

Abbey of St. Denis, 45
Abbey of St. Germain,
  89
Abbots of Cluny, 86
Académie Française,
  102-4
Aix-la-Chapelle, 110
Amboise, Jacques d', 87
Antin, Marquis of, 44
Apaches, 64-66
Apartments, 89-93
Arc de Triomphe, 117,
  119-22
Arc of triumph,
  Napoleonic, 107
Artois, Comte d', 125
Attila, 80
Auteuil, 36, 59
Avenue de la Grande
  Armée, 122-23
Avenue de l'Obsérva-
  toire, 89
Avenue du Bois de
  Boulogne, 123
Avenue Nicholas II, 118

Bagatelle, Château de,
  125-27
Bartholdi, 130
Basilica of the Sacred
  Heart, 44
Bastille, 45-48, 55, 57, 89
Bateaux Mouches (Fly
  Boats), 59-61
Baths
  apartments offering,
    90-93
  of Roman palace, 88

Besant, Annie, 84
Bibliothèque Ste.
  Geneviève, 35, 79-80
Bismarck, Otto von, 114
Blavatsky, Helena
  Petrovna, 85
Bohemianism, 97-98
Bois de Boulogne, 122,
  123, 124-27
Boni de Castellane, M. le
  Comte, 123
Bordeaux, statues repre-
  senting, 113
Boulevards, 37, 44-45,
  56
Boulevard St. Germain,
  88, 89, 98
Bouquinistes, 104
Brest, statues represent-
  ing, 113
Bulwarks, 44

Cabaret du Néant, 36
Caesar's Tower, 69
Café de la Paix, 38-41, 62
Chamber of Deputies, 47
Champs-Élysées, 116-18,
  123
Charenton, 59
Charles IX, 70
Charles X, 46, 108, 125
Chelles, Jean de, 75
Cité, La. *See* Isle de la
  Cité, L'
City Hall. *See* Hôtel de
  Ville
Clotilde, Queen, 80
Clovis, King, 80

College of France, 78
Comédie Française, La.
  See National Conser-
  vatory of Dramatic
  Art
Commune, 46, 75-76,
  108-9
Communists, 50, 57
Conciergerie, 70
Constituant Assembly,
  111
Corday, Charlotte, 112
Corsica, 109, 131, 135
Curie, Marie, 84-85
Curie, Pierre, 84

Damiens, 57
Danton, 112
Delair, Frédéric, 100-101
Desmoulins, Camille, 55-
  57
De Sommerard, 87
Dôme des Invalides, 132,
  134
Domrémy, 53
Dreyfus, Alfred, 103

Ecole des Beaux-Arts,
  L', 78
Eiffel Tower, 131
Esplanade des Invalides,
  118, 131-32
Eugénie, Empress, 75,
  108
Evans, Dr., 108
Exposition of 1900, 118

Fête de Neuilly, 123

Fishermen, 64
Franco-Prussian War, 108, 113
French Revolution, 45-48, 55, 63, 81, 87, 107-8, 113

Garden of the Luxembourg, 85
Geneviève, Ste., 80-81
Grand Opera House, 41-44, 50
Grand Palais des Beaux-Arts, Le, 118
Grand Prix, 127-28
Grands Boulevards. See Boulevards
Grand Trianon, Le, 123
Guillotin, Dr., 111
Guillotine, 111-12

Henri IV, 57, 63
Henry of Navarre, 49, 63
Hôtel des Invalides, 132
Hôtel de Ville, 57-58, 75-76
Hotel Ritz, 36
Hugo, Victor, 82
Huguenots, 69-70

Institute of France, 61, 101-4
Isle de la Cité, L', 59, 62, 63, 66-77
Isle des Treilles, L', 63
Isle St. Louis, 59, 67

Jardin Henri IV, 62-64

Jeanne d'Arc, 52-53
Josephine, Empress, 75
Julian, 87-88
July Column, 45-46
July Revolution, 46, 49

Latin Quarter, 36, 59, 78-85, 89-90, 94
Left bank, 78
Lettres-de-cachet, 47
Lille, statues representing, 113
Longchamps, 36, 127-30
Louis, Dr., 111
Louis, Saint. See Louis IX
Louis IX, 68, 69, 71, 79
Louis XI, 57
Louis XIV, 44, 105, 123, 132
Louis XV, 55, 57, 110
Louis XVI, 107-8
Louis XVIII, 108
Louis Philippe ("Citizen King"), 46, 49, 108, 112, 122
Louvre, 36, 60, 104-7
  Garden of the, 107
Lowe, Sir Hudson, 134
Lutetia, 66
Lyons, statues representing, 113

Maintenon, Mme. de, 123
Maisons-Laffitte, 36
Marais, Le, 96-97
Marat, 48

Marie Antoinette, 70, 108, 112, 125
Marseilles, statues representing, 113
Maxim's, 36
Medici, Catherine de', 70, 107
Molière, 102
Montmartre, 35, 44
Montparnasse, 35
Morgue, 76-77
Moulin Rouge, 36
Musée de Cluny, 86-88
Musset, Alfred de, 54

Nantes, statues representing, 113
Napoleon, Arch of. See Arc de Triomphe; Napoleonic arch of triumph
Napoleon III, 50, 75, 108
Napoleon Bonaparte, 48-50, 63, 75, 108, 109, 117, 122, 131-36
Napoleonic arch of triumph, 107
National Academy of Music. See Grand Opera House
National Conservatory of Dramatic Art, 53-54
New Bridge. See Pont Neuf
News Kiosks, 38-39
"Nick Carter Tales," 64-65

Notre Dame, 61, 72-77

Obelisk of Luxor, 114-16, 117
Outer Boulevards, 36

Paillard's, 36
Palace of the Caesars, 87
Palais de Justice, 68-72
Palais de l'Industrie, 118
Palais Royal, 55-57
Palissy, Bernard, 89
Panthéon, 61, 81-82
Père Lachaise, 48
Petit Palais, Le, 118
Philip, King, 58
Philippe Égalité, 55, 112
Place de Grève, 57-58
Place de la Bastille, 45-46
Place de la Concorde, 47, 107, 110-16
Place de l'Etoile, 122
Place de l'Opéra, 37
Place du Carrousel, 107
Place du Parvis Notre Dame, La, 73
Place Rivoli, 52
Place Vendôme, 49-50, 63
Pont Alexandre III, 118
Pont de la Concorde, 47
Pont des Arts, 104
Pont Neuf, 49, 61-63
Pont St. Louis, 67
Porte des Ternes, 130
Porte Maillot, 123
Porte St. Denis, 44-45
Pozzo di Borgo, 109

Quai Henri IV, 67
Quartier Latin. *See* Latin Quarter

Ramses II, King, 114-16, 117
Ravaillac, 57
Reign of Terror, 58, 108, 110-12
Restoration, 49, 108
Revolutionists of 1830, 108
Revolution of 1848, 108
Richelieu, Cardinal, 79, 102
Robespierre, 58, 112
Rodin, 82-83
Rouen, statues representing, 113
Rousseau, 82
Rue Brise Miche, La, 97
Rue de la Chaussée d'Antin, 44
Rue de la Paix, 36, 51-52, 56
Rue de Rivoli, 52

Sacred Relics, 72
St. Antoine, 48
St. Bartholomew, 69-70
St. Etienne-du-Mont, 80-81
St. Germain-des-Prés, 89
St. Germain l'Auxerrois, 69-70
St. Helena, 131, 132-34, 135
St. Louis-des-Invalides, 132
St. Peter's, 49
Sainte Chapelle, 71-72
Salle des Pas-Perdus, 70-71
School of Mines, 78
Seine, 59-64, 69, 77-78, 80, 104, 110, 112, 118, 131
Sèvres, 89
Silver Tower, 69
Sorbon, Robert of, 79
Sorbonne, 35, 78-79
Strasbourg monument, 113-14
Swedenborg, Emanuel, 84
Swiss Guard, 108

Talleyrand (née Anna Gould), Mme. la Duchesse de, 123
Telegraph system, 93
Telephone system, 93
Thackeray, William Makepeace, 99
Théâtre du Palais Royal, 56-57
Théâtre Française, La. *See* National Conservatory of Dramatic Art
"Thinker, The" (Rodin), 82-83
Thirion, 98-100
Tondeurs de chiens, 64
Tour d'Argent, La, 100-101

Tour de l'Horloge, 69
Tower of St. Jacques, 59,
   61
Trajan Column, 49
Tuileries
   Garden of the, 107,
      110
   Palace of the, 60, 75,
      107-9, 135

University of Paris, 79

Vendôme Column, 48-
   50, 63
Venus de Milo, 36
Versailles, 107, 109, 120,
   123
Violet-le-Duc, 74
Voltaire, 82

Wallace, Sir Richard,
   125, 127
William the Great, 120

Zola, Emile, 102-4